Remote

Remote

Finding Home *in the* Bitterroots

DJ Lee

Oregon State University Press   Corvallis

Library of Congress Cataloging-in-Publication Data

Names: Lee, Debbie (Debbie Jean), 1960– author.
Title: Remote : finding home in the Bitterroots / D.J. Lee.
Other titles: Finding home in the Bitterroots
Description: Corvallis, [OR] : Oregon State University Press, [2020] | "Moose
    Creek Ranger Station."
Identifiers: LCCN 2019054420 | ISBN 9780870710001 ; (trade pbk. ; alk. paper) |
    ISBN 9780870710049
Subjects: LCSH: Lee, Debbie (Debbie Jean), 1960—Family. | Selway-Bitterroot
    Wilderness (Idaho and Mont.)—Biography. | Johnson, Connie, approximately
    1942– | Missing persons—Selway-Bitterroot Wilderness (Idaho and Mont.) |
    Women park rangers—Selway-Bitterroot Wilderness (Idaho and Mont.)—Biog-
    raphy. | Outdoor life—Selway-Bitterroot Wilderness (Idaho and Mont.) | Wil-
    derness area users—Selway-Bitterroot Wilderness (Idaho and Mont.)—Biogra-
    phy. | Selway-Bitterroot Wilderness (Idaho and Mont.)—Description and travel.
Classification: LCC F752.I2 L44 2020 | DDC 978.6/89—dc23
LC record available at https://lccn.loc.gov/2019054420

♾ This paper meets the requirements of ANSI/NISO Z39.48-1992
(Permanence of Paper).

Part of chapter 9 was published in *Narrative Magazine* (2014); part of chapter 21
was published in *Silk Road Review* 15 (2016).

Oregon State University
OSU Press

Oregon State University Press
121 The Valley Library
Corvallis OR 97331-4501
541-737-3166 • fax 541-737-3170
www.osupress.oregonstate.edu

For Shirley Case Wagoner

During the last fifteen years, I often asked myself why I was writing this book. I see now I was writing with you in mind. I've always wanted to be like you, how you forgive so easily, how you see the good in people. I love your tenacity, your complexity, your mystery. Mom, this book is for you.

Our place is part of who we are.
—Gary Snyder, *The Practice of the Wild*

Ghosts and writers meet in their concern for the past.
—W. G. Sebald, *Campo Santo*

Contents

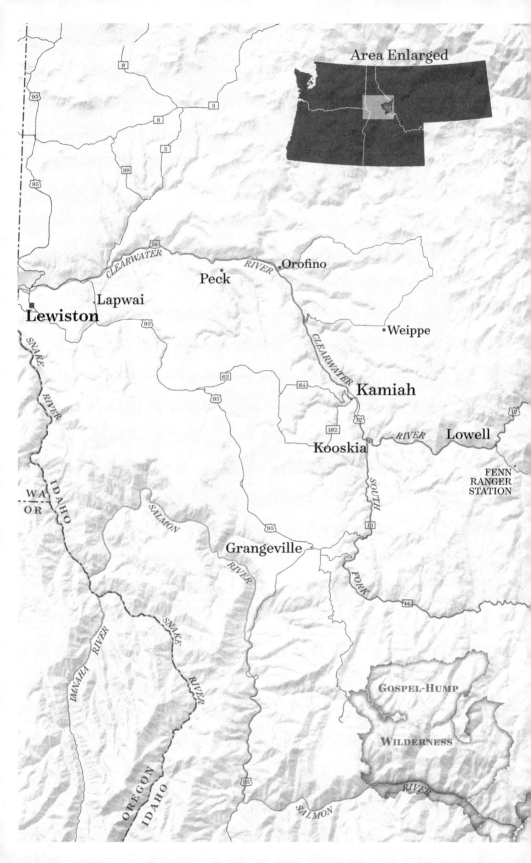

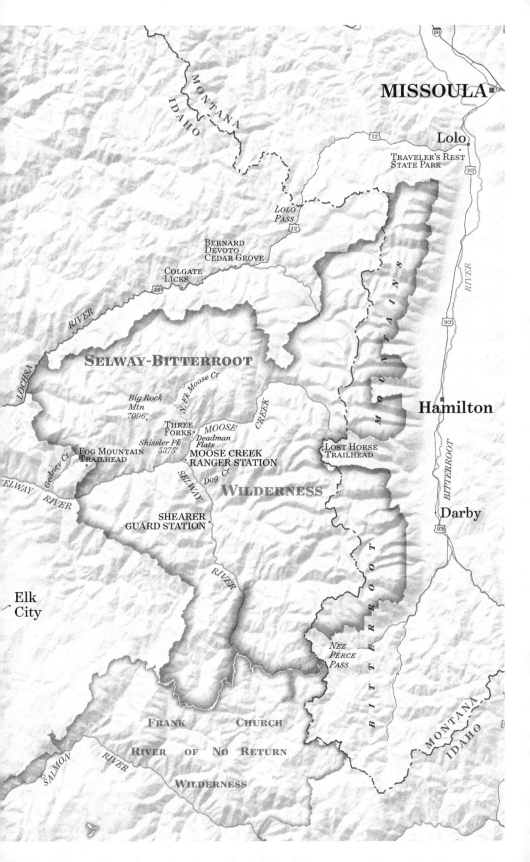

1 Bridge

October 10, 2018

My phone buzzes, and I pick up. It's my father.

"Did you know Connie went missing?" he asks. I hear his metallic voice through the speaker, but the meaning slides and blurs, is lost.

"You've got the wrong person," I say to my father. An image of Connie's husband, a rugged mule skinner who died three months ago of a heart attack, flashes before me. "It's Lloyd who's missing."

"No," my father says. "It's Connie."

I'm at home in Moscow, Idaho—low sun through big windows, leaves tumbling across the lawn—but my mind flies away to Connie, who should be ninety miles south in the tiny town of Nezperce or at one of the ranger stations where she volunteers along the Selway or Lochsa Rivers. "Maybe she's just late. She'll be back." I say this, but I'm lightheaded, unable to stand. I stagger to a chair and sit. My father mumbles something to my mother and hands her the phone.

"Connie's been missing for more than a week," she says in a flat voice. "It's in the papers. She and her dog Ace. They both vanished in the Selway-Bitterroot."

I stand and head to my laptop, where a Google search turns up dozens of entries. I click an article: "Search efforts are underway for seventy-six-year-old Connie Johnson, who was working as the cook at a hunting camp in the Fog Mountain area of the Selway-Bitterroot Wilderness." Skimming down, I see the Idaho County sheriff's official statement: "Honestly, we don't know what happened."

It doesn't make sense. No one understands the Selway-Bitterroot better than Connie. No one knows its valleys and creeks, meadows and peaks, moose and bear, kingfishers and thrush, salmon and trout as she does. No one knows what's buried there in more detail than she.

"It's very sad," my mother says, voice trailing away. "You know what they say? If you want to disappear, you go to Idaho County."

My mother is right. The Selway-Bitterroot is one of the most remote places left in America. The federally protected wilderness drapes across the Idaho-Montana border in the northern Rocky Mountains, where it's joined to the Frank Church River of No Return Wilderness and the Gospel Hump Wilderness to form the largest area of roadless land in the contiguous United States.

I own several maps of the Selway-Bitterroot, and on each one the wilderness is a splash of green—thick and bulbous to the south, tapering to a neat stem in the north. I've also flown over it dozens of times in small planes. From that angle, the land appears exposed and pulsating, canyons and mountains like ripples and convolutions of a human brain. In spring and summer, it's like the nervous system of a giant being, as the whole region melts down mountainsides and through ravines to the Lochsa and Selway Rivers.

Hundreds of trails snake through the Selway-Bitterroot, with scores of access points, some expansive with horse corrals and vehicle parking, some just a pull off on a dirt patch, and a few dark and secret with one spot for a tent. I've been there—sometimes camping overnight next to a trailhead, sometimes striking out on foot for a few miles, sometimes going deeper—with fires raging and smoke thick as fog, in crotch-deep snow or under curtains of rain, and in the mellow seasons, late spring and early fall, when the land is waking up or going to sleep. But to Connie, this place is home.

⟿

My family has been connected to the Selway-Bitterroot for nearly a century, but I never set foot there until I was almost forty-five years old. I've spent the past fifteen years trying to piece together the history of the wilderness and of my grandparents, who lived there for decades. The memory of those years is like the Selway River itself. What seems to be a singular waterway is actually hundreds of streams and creeks, each with its own course, its own confluence. The watersheds of Halfway,

Meeker, Marten, Three Links, Bear, Mink, and Moose Creeks feed the Selway in large flows. The shallower drainages of Puzzle, Lone Pine, Coyote, Pinchot, Wolf, Ballinger, Power, and Cupboard Creeks add significant volume to the river. Jack, Bar, Cascade, and Hidden Creeks—as well as dozens of other unnamed streams, rivulets, becks, seeps, and dribbles—are smaller, some drying up completely in summer, but they still contribute to the river. On a map, I can trace the thick, ropey Selway just as I can follow the river of my memory, but when I look more closely, I see them both as braided currents, their true power flowing from convergences.

Connie is one of these connections. She and I are not related by blood, but she's become a towering figure in my life. Connie is thin and tall, much taller than I am, and she's twenty years older. Every time I see her, she seems to be wearing a "Life Is Good" T-shirt, her silky blonde hair styled in a bob. I remember walking a trail with her along the Selway River some twelve years ago, the forest thick with cedar, pine, and fir, me thick with admiration for her, the air thick with scents of green. We came to something shiny and white lying on the ground. A laminated sign that read: "The bridge at Dog Creek is out." Connie scooped it up and turned to me.

"Look, it was attached with teeny tiny staples," she said in a brisk voice, scowling. The sign had other warnings in a smaller font. "Beware of high water."

Connie looked perturbed, but I couldn't understand why.

She tugged some twine from the pocket of her jeans and cut it with a knife strapped to her belt. She had the strongest hands I'd ever seen on a woman. She rifled through brush along the trail and pulled out a long, thick branch.

"Where do you cross if the bridge is out?" I asked naïvely.

"You don't cross!" Her arms flew out, hands palms up. "The bridge is gone, swept away in spring runoff. That means the trail's impassable." The curl of her mouth said she wanted to laugh at me, but she didn't. She had been a Spanish teacher in Iowa before she became a wilderness ranger, and she treated the landscape as her giant classroom. "You could try to find a fallen tree and shimmy across on your butt. That's dangerous, though. Or you could go down to the mouth of Dog Creek and into the

Selway River. But you'd get wet, and in high water, if the bridge is out, you don't do that either."

Connie and I were not planning to cross Dog Creek, thank God, but others might have been. She finished tying the sign to the stick, shoved it in the ground with one big heave, and stepped back to assess if it would be visible to backpackers, horse and mule people, trail crew, firefighters.

"That'll do it," she said.

⌁

My father gets back on the phone.

"Maybe she's lost," I say halfheartedly. But I can't really imagine Connie lost. She knows every inch of trail in that place.

"Not a chance," he says. "She never did bushwhack." My father has accompanied her on several volunteer trips, and like everyone, he holds on to her every word. "I heard her say one time, *I'm not one to strike out overland.*"

"But what if she had to?" I reply. "What if the trail was impassable?"

"Well, I don't know," he says.

When we hang up, I stand and remember, bare feet planted on the mellow hardwood, twenty-foot bookcases crammed with thousands of pages of research about the Selway-Bitterroot Wilderness looming behind me.

After Connie repaired the Dog Creek warning sign that day, I asked her why she did it. Trail maintenance, restoring backcountry ranger stations, organizing intern trainings, cooking for hunters. I said, "Why do you keep coming back even though you're retired?"

"You know," she said, "as much as I try to get involved with my community in Nezperce, in the library and all that, I just can't. These are my people, wilderness people. But the real reason is the wilderness itself."

I didn't understand then how wilderness could be its own reason for returning. But after I met Connie, I, too, couldn't quit.

Why can't I stop?

The sheriff's words linger in my mind.

Honestly, we don't know.

2 Message in a Bottle

"Deserted Cook May Be Alive" reads the headline of a *New York Times* story printed in December 1893. The cook in question was George Colgate, who was abandoned in the Bitterroots a few months earlier by the hunting party who had hired him.

George Colgate was my first literary introduction to the Selway-Bitterroot Wilderness. I read the *Times* article, along with an 1895 pam-

George Colgate's grave, 1904. George Elmer Ritchey photo. Courtesy of Manuscripts, Archives, and Special Collections, Washington State University Libraries.

phlet written by one of the hunters, in a bookstore near my home in Moscow some eighteen years ago. I recall how, as I sat in the overstuffed chair sipping coffee, I was visited by an uncanny feeling that Colgate was part of my own lineage. I attributed the feeling partly to the fact that though the hunting party hailed from New York, Colgate resided in Post Falls, a ten-minute drive from Spokane Valley, where my parents live, and partly to the inexplicable glitches in the narrative.

The tale is riveting: A group of wealthy men from New York, who saw the Bitterroots as a playground for big game trophy hunting, enlisted Colgate as a cook, not knowing he had an enlarged prostate and a chronic bladder infection for which he used a catheter. They therefore had no idea he left that catheter behind when he set out with the expedition. Although the hunters engaged guides and met mountain men and members of the Nimíipuu, they suffered from a series of bad decisions, extreme weather, and terrible luck, none so severe as the flare-up of Colgate's bladder infection. Without his catheter, Colgate's legs bloated and putrefied, and he lost his ability to walk. The hunters, who ultimately survived the ordeal, claimed that the cook also lost his mind, at which point they left him on the banks of the Lochsa River. When the hunters stumbled out of the mountains and told their tale, people were outraged.

That outrage was chronicled in newspapers across the country. Journalists shamed the hunters for weeks. And then the *Times* article appeared, offering some hope. Colgate's name was found on a message in a bottle, a message that read in part:

> Bitter Root Mountains. I am alive. Tell them to come and get me as soon as any one finds this. I am fifty miles from civilization, as near as I can tell. I am George Colgate, one of the lost Carlin Party. My legs are better. I can walk some. Take this to the St. Elmo Hotel, Kendrick, Idaho, and you will be liberally rewarded. My name is George Colgate, from Post Falls. This bottle came by me one day and I caught it, and write these words to take me out. George Colgate. Good-by, wife and children.

Of the hundreds of disappearances in the Selway-Bitterroot—dead ends, red herrings, and freaky unknowns I've learned about through the years—Colgate's story entered me like a desire. Rarely do I visit and not see visions of the deserted cook crawling from a snow hole with a whiskey bottle wedged under his chin. I see his clothes scabbed to his skin; I smell his desperation as he kneels by the river with shaky hands and sends that bottle adrift. Like the biblical ark, the bottle holds a sacred message. It bobs in the current, lodges in a snow-covered logjam, dislodges in a moment of melt, and floats from the Lochsa to the Clearwater to the Snake River. There, another man, wearing an oilskin coat, coaxes it ashore and carries it to the St. Elmo Hotel.

At the St. Elmo, where Colgate bunked before embarking with the hunters, authorities confirm that the signature on the message matches Colgate's signature on the hotel registry. No fewer than seven search and rescue parties strike out through the cedars and pines, over mountains, through gorges, but they run into terrible difficulties. In one search party, several men die in a raging river. Colgate's son, part of another rescue mission, is crushed under a falling tree, though miraculously he survives. They find nothing. Later, an army expedition stumbles upon human remains eight miles from where Colgate was supposedly abandoned.

To this day, no one knows how Colgate ended, or if his bones are truly laid to rest. Still, the Forest Service has commemorated the abandoned cook. At mile 122 on Highway 12, a roadside memorial gapes like a mouth that can almost speak: Colgate Licks.

I've passed Colgate Licks dozens of times. Only once, on a late fall afternoon, did I stop and saunter along the nature trail in half-forest, half-meadow. An eerie feeling came over me as I stood on the edge of the massive wilderness that swallows people whole. One nearby sign explained that "licks" are favored by ungulates, who paw the earth to get potassium, magnesium, and zinc to rise to the surface, and then they chew the soil. I remember how gruesome the name sounded as I imagined elk and moose ingesting Colgate along with the dirt. But later, I saw Colgate's fate as the most sacred of afterlives.

There are places like Colgate Licks throughout the wilderness, stories bled into the very ground, cycled and recycled through other living things. But I have never been able to shake the feeling that there is something suspicious about Colgate's narrative. Take the 1895 pamphlet, written by one of the hunters, detailing the account of the cook as he was being deserted: "Although Colgate's head was turned toward us, he made no motion or outcry as he saw us disappear, one by one, around the bend." I suspect the hunter isn't telling the truth. Colgate's note is even more disturbing. It is the repetition: "I am George Colgate." The insistence seems unnatural, an overeagerness to convince. The good-bye to his wife and children is the strangest of all, as if the writer of the note knew Colgate was already gone. But the bigger question is why people, myself included, are drawn to what has disappeared in the wilderness.

3   Esther

My maternal grandmother didn't want me to call her Grandma. "My name's not Grandma," she'd say, raising her chin like a proud horse. "Call me Esther."

I loved the name Esther, the brave Jewish queen of the Old Testament. Esther, meaning "star" and "hidden or concealed," both of which fit my grandmother perfectly. Esther was my caregiver, the one who taught me to read and encouraged me to write. It was Esther who first told me about the wilderness, who urged me to walk through the land only after she was gone, and once I did, who kept reaching from the other side and pulling me back in.

From my early teens until she died in 1999, I talked with my grandmother every week by phone, comforted by her quiet attention and soft *um-hums*. To this day, I see her leaning next to her Wedgewood stove, hip steadied on the metal side, black wall phone in her hand with the long receiver cord curlicued at her feet. Esther's feet were larger than all twelve siblings in her family, yet the only shoes she owned were hand-me-downs from those sisters and brothers.

Esther Squires Case, 1925. Family photo.

She had no choice but to squeeze into them like a Cinderella's stepsister until her bones folded back on themselves. Her deformed feet reminded her of her childhood poverty, which I knew about from what my mother told me. My grandmother never related such things on our phone calls. Instead, our discussions centered on my difficulties at school, the jealousies, intimacies, and heartbreaks of friendships and romances, or the movies I saw, books I read. Her only agenda seemed to be helping me form a sense of self.

Moments with my grandmother contrasted with those in my family, when I often felt overshadowed by three brothers and loquacious parents—my parents never tired of talking about what was external to them. Dinner hours were filled with speculation about the motives behind a neighbor's or politician's words or behaviors, or lengthy backstories about landmarks and events—the history of Chief Seattle's statue at Tilikum Place or the social significance of the Watergate trials. With Esther, I could be heard, because Esther was a listening kind of person.

Every summer, our family left our home in Seattle, drove across Washington State, wound around Chatcolet Lake in Northern Idaho, and arrived at Esther's in the tiny town of St. Maries. I watched as my grandmother and my mother pulled up chairs, faces inches apart in a shared space speaking a shared language. I loved the pure music of their talk, the art of their soft bodies leaning toward one another. While they gossiped, Esther let me paw through her house, which was so different from my mother, who kept her things private, tucked away in locked drawers and cabinets. My grandmother had no such boundaries. Like an animal chewing earth for life-giving minerals, I dug up everything I could in her higgledy-piggledy house. Musty books, metal boxes, nickels and pennies that had been flattened on a train track, a jeweled pincushion, a scrap of lavender velvet.

My grandmother's objects held vibrant power, especially those she bequeathed to me and let me cart back to Seattle. The tortoise shell comb, the string of faux pearls, the soiled lace doily gave me comfort when my mother and I fought. Our struggles began, at least to my teenage mind, the day my mother brought me home from the hospital. She told the story of my homecoming so often I sometimes believed it was my own memory. She walked in the door after giving birth and found two rocking chairs, a small one designed for a toddler and a regular-sized one for rocking a real baby. My father had purchased the small one, an imitation Windsor with high back and carved spindles, at Sears for twenty dollars, a significant amount for a penniless young couple—just nineteen—living in Lewiston, Idaho, in 1960. The adult rocker he found at Goodwill; it was covered in three layers of paint and springs poked through the seat. My mother loved her new baby, of course, but she was also hurt that my father would bestow on their newborn an expensive chair and saddle her with a secondhand rocker. I always envisioned myself in that shoebox-sized apartment, a blurry larva teetering on the sofa, already sensing the tensions drawn across the fabric of our family. I also imagined my parents, my mother's long blue-black hair roped into a braid and hanging down her back and her dark, fighting eyes, and my father's red beard framing his thin Irish face, his auburn eyebrows lifted in confusion, tripping over himself to console my mother.

By the time I reached my teens, my mother and I were finding it difficult to live peaceably in the same space, not an uncommon problem for mothers and daughters, except our fights were disturbingly frequent and volatile—screaming, crying, hitting, vowing to never speak again. The summer I was sixteen, our conflicts grew so grave that my father threatened to kick me out of the house, and so, in what I see now as an act of compassion as much as desperation, my mother put me on a Greyhound bus in Seattle. Three hundred fifty miles later I was in rural Idaho sitting on Esther's front lawn eating ripe peaches and listening to a chorus of crickets. The next morning, I put on my bikini and pranced out to lie in the sun. Esther quickly came out and stared at me with arched brow and pursed lips, and I saw I wasn't going to get away with my delinquent habits—the smoking, drinking, boyfriends, and parties. She told me her raspberries needed picking, pushed a wide-brimmed hat on my head, and sent me out to work.

I found myself in my grandmother's employ every day that summer. I grew to love the structure of harvesting lettuce and carrots and peas, mowing the lawn, and delivering meals to shut-ins. What gave me the most joy was helping her sort through the junk at the thrift store that she ran. Old curtains and tea cups and piles of clothing, broken plates and silverware, hundreds of books and records, malfunctioning radios and small auto parts, plastic bags full of buttons or zippers or paper clips. Used but still useful things holding the patina of other lives. After a while, we began taking home out-of-fashion garments, which we'd redesign into something I could wear. A dress with a full circle skirt became a halter-top, a rabbit-fur collar turned into trim for jeans and wool hats. We repurposed other things, too. An iron was remade into a doorstop. Heavy goblets transformed into planters for walnut tree seedlings. It was a summer of resurrection.

In Esther's attic, painted mint green, a crawl space with a secret door ran along one entire wall. There I found some 16 mm films, which I knew from previous visits had belonged to my grandfather George, though I didn't know anything about him. He died when I was two and a half. The films, some cut into small pieces of two or three frames, were rolled into tin cans. I opened them one hot afternoon, hoping for a glimpse of my mother or grandmother or grandfather, but when I held the strips up to the light all I saw were embryonic blobs dotting each frame.

A few days before I was to return to Seattle, in the grips of a sharp, giddy feeling that lives in the seam between leaving and having left, we sat in her living room. I was scanning her bookshelves, as I often did, when I spotted something I'd never seen: a black photo book. I slid it from the shelf. As I opened to an image of her family, a heavy silence grew between us. Esther, a little brown-haired girl with a rag bow in her hair, stood among her twelve brothers and sisters, her mother, Mary, and her father, Edward. Edward, tall and lanky in dirty overalls and with a huge mustache concealing his mouth, looked like a scarecrow.

But he was much more. My mother often told the story of how Edward had set up a hydraulic gold mine in the north Idaho hills above Kooskia, believing he would strike it rich, while Mary birthed one child after another. "Every time she got pregnant," my mother said, "she hung her head in shame." Food was scarce. If, on occasion, there was a piece of venison or rabbit meat, Edward would take it all for himself, while the children got broth and bread, or nothing at all. When Edward didn't find gold, he extravagantly bought a typewriter, tapping out short stories and movie scripts he intended to sell like his idol, F. Scott Fitzgerald. His writing career failed, and he sank into depression and didn't get out of bed for nearly two years.

I militated against my mother's version of my great-grandfather's life, irritated when she brought it up, because she seemed to emphasize Edward's insensitivity and self-absorption, while I clung to his artist-dreamer sensibility, the part I liked to think Esther had inherited and passed down to me. Where else would my obsession with narrative come from?

On a subsequent page was George, a shocking image that seemed to hold something big and important. But what? A man in his early twenties in 1925, he stood on a tree stump holding a full bear skin with head attached. His short, wiry body and sharp jawline gave him a defiant look. It was the most provocative image I'd seen in my life; to think I was related to this person, that Esther had been married to him, and my mother raised by him. He seemed a foreigner, the dramatic opposite of the depressed, creative Edward. The more I looked at the photo of George against the scraggly forest background, engulfed by the bear skin, the more I seemed to need to know about him.

I remember how when I asked about him, Esther folded her arms across her chest and said, "There's not much to say." It was so unlike her to stonewall, to shut down, and I was hurt, having been immersed in her openness all summer. When I pressed her, she let slip that he'd been a ranger in the Bitterroot wilderness. From then on, the words "Bitterroot," "wilderness," and "grandfather" were cemented for me, though I'd never been in a wilderness and had not even seen a photo of my grandfather until that moment. But I thought he must be very important to be surrounded by such silence, and I invested him with the power of the forbidden.

Esther got up, and George and the wilderness entered my life with the rustle of her jeans as she shuffled away.

Esther, star. Queen of concealment.

It was the last time I saw the photographs for many years, and when I returned to Seattle and my family, glowing from a summer of loving attention, I had all but forgotten them.

4 Lost Horse

In countless excursions to the Selway-Bitterroot over the past decade, I've entered from trailheads in Montana and Idaho: Flat Creek, Wilderness Gateway, Blodgett Canyon, Warm Springs, Gedney Creek, and Elk Summit, to name a few. But Lost Horse, located thirty miles southwest of Hamilton, Montana, has a peculiar magic.

Lost Horse, at six thousand feet of elevation, is where prospectors crossed in 1881 in high water and their horses drowned.

Trail from Lost Horse, 1969. Dick Walker photo.

Lost Horse is the jagged edge of the Bitterroot Divide.

Lost Horse, where I went five years after my grandmother died, is my first and most important portal.

I remember how sluggishly our Ford F150 pickup crawled up Lost Horse Road on that hot August afternoon. Joe—our driver, our fixer, our pilot—slowed to ten miles per hour as the road turned to gravel and narrowed. Joe operated a shuttle service out of Hamilton flying people into and out of the Selway-Bitterroot or transporting them to trailheads. All four of us—my father, Myron, Joe, and I—sat hip to hip across one front seat. Myron, my husband, tall and broad-shouldered, silently took it all in, as was his way, while my father commented on the road, its steep grades, dips and humps over boulders, blind turns, and loose rocks the size of footballs, as if articulating my own thoughts. My father and I noticed the same things just as we resembled one another with our fair skin, hazel eyes, and broom of reddish-brown hair, though his was platinum by then. We'd both chosen vocations—plumber and literature professor—of subterranean labor, his in pipes underground and behind walls, mine in meaning beneath words. We both gravitated toward extremes. My mother often said, "Being married to your father is so intense." She may very well have commented to him about me, "Being her mother is so intense."

Compared to my father and Myron, Joe appeared small, even petite. A man of fifty at the time, he seemed like the silent type, but in fact he loved to talk, and his favorite subject was the land in front of us. Joe explained that the Nimíipuu had lived in the Bitterroots for over twelve thousand years. They had used, and still use, a network of trails for gathering, hunting, fishing, vision quests, and ceremonies, a network far more complex than what Lewis and Clark saw on their trek in 1805 and the Forest Service had since codified. "Ya know," Joe said as he shifted the manual gear, "people think of wilderness as a Jack London book, but there's so much history here."

"There's so much history everywhere," I said flippantly, hearing the cliché instead of something with true meaning. Joe responded apologetically that he wasn't a scholar or anything like that. I felt the sting of my thoughtless rebuke and went back to staring out the window.

I saw a golden lab was running up the road toward us. Then three hikers in full backpack gear appeared, waving their poles. Joe stopped and we piled out into the dusty air. The lab shoved her head into my crotch, whipping her tail against my thigh.

"We don't know whose dog this is," the hikers yelled, still twenty feet away. "She seems lost."

Joe rubbed his mustache. He wore a stonewashed blue T-shirt and faded Levi's from which the waistband of red boxers crept. I wondered if it was a look he cultivated, meant to add Western charm to the silver-fox appeal he already had. "It's not our dog," he said when the hikers reached us, winded.

"We can't take the dog," one of them said, as all seven of us stood in a loose circle, eyes pleading with one another for someone to volunteer to take the dog. She had little round eyebrows raised in pure hope.

"I'm driving these folks up to Lost Horse," Joe said. "Then I'm going back to Hamilton."

Myron scratched the dog's neck. I could see his mind turning. "Could you bring her to a shelter?" he said.

Joe looked at the ground. *"Wellllllll."* He drew the word out in steel strands and pointed toward the lab's nice leather collar. "She obviously belongs to someone."

My father looked at his watch. Already 4:00 p.m. Joe shifted back and forth on his feet, hands plunged into his pockets. He motioned us with his chin and we crawled back into the truck cab. I turned and watched the hikers and the dog fade from view. What would happen to her? Would she wander the road hungry for days until she perished? Would Joe take her on his way down? Maybe the hikers would let her come with them after all. Or she'd make her way home, wherever home was.

As we got back on the road, Joe mentioned Connie. It was the first time I heard her name, and I recall clearly that he spoke about her as if she were a celebrity, as if everyone knew who she was and we should too. She was the wilderness ranger at Moose Creek Ranger Station. Connie: the woman I now see as vital to what I know about the Selway-Bitterroot. It's odd for me to think there was a time I didn't know Connie's name, just as it's strange to imagine not knowing Moose Creek Ranger Station. Moose Creek: the place my grandparents had once lived, the very place

Myron, my father, and I would hike to over the next week. I casually jotted *Connie* in my notebook, someone I might later contact for information. But even then, probably because of Joe's hyperbolic description, there was something more: a curious pull, a need to know Connie, a tug not unlike what I'd felt when I glimpsed the image of my grandfather in Esther's photo book.

The land was dappled in sun and shadows, and the crunch of gravel under the tires meditative, though I noticed with some apprehension the road growing narrower and steeper, an angular rock face on one side and a sloping cliff on the other. We turned a corner and met another truck head on. Joe pulled to the cliff side of the road, a two-hundred-foot drop. The thought of tumbling over the edge weakened my knees.

The truck stopped and a man rolled down the window. "Did you see a dog?" he said. As Joe gave him directions to find the hiking group, Myron squeezed my hand—dog and owner would be reunited.

Soon, we were making the final pull up the grade to Lost Horse Trailhead, which I had imagined would be dense and moody and steep. In reality the terrain was flat, covered in furry bear grass and a riot of alpine flowers and shrubs. Joe parked next to Twin Lakes, two kidney-shaped bodies of water. The lakes created an opening in the forest into which late-afternoon light poured, turning the water gemstone clear. The forest shimmered and seemed to tremble. It was tender and beautiful and alarming, as when, in a dream, you can hold two or three mind states in one scene.

Myron, an engineer, and my father had spent hours with the Selway-Bitterroot topographical maps measuring, calculating, predicting, and planning for every possible difficulty we might encounter in the fifty miles to Moose Creek Ranger Station. They pranced around the gravel lot, animated as we unloaded our backpacks and poles and they took a gear inventory. I held back. I should have felt riveted with excitement, full of joy, and I did, but I was also a little nauseated from nerves. I'd never been on a long backpack or in a vast roadless land. Physically, I was sure I'd be okay. Psychologically, I wasn't sure at all. The wilderness, the place I had known about since I was sixteen, the place I had felt a strange homesickness for but had never seen, was thick with meaning.

Whenever I conjure that hike from Lost Horse, I immediately see myself five years earlier, just a few months after my grandmother died, sitting beside my mother in a Safeway parking lot, salmon, broccoli, and a case of diet soda filling the back seat of my car. And whenever I think of my mother and myself in that parking lot, Lost Horse Trailhead springs to mind, because I heard about Lost Horse for the first time in that lot.

I remember the errand to Safeway with my mother felt so unusual because we were rarely alone together. As I started the engine and began to back up, she said, "When I was thirteen, my parents planned a big wilderness adventure going back to my dad's old homestead in the Selway-Bitterroot." Her eyes grew big and hard, and her voice quivered. I pulled back in and shut off the engine, knowing she was telling me something important. "I don't know if my dad's homestead buildings were still standing in nineteen fifty-four, but Mother, Barbara, and I had planned a trip back there with Dad." That she'd been to the edge of the wilderness, and that George actually owned property there—a homestead—was completely unknown to me then, and I felt the power of the revelation.

"We drove to Lost Horse Trailhead, and there was ice on the ground—that's how cold it was in May, but I didn't care. I was so excited." The family would be in the wilderness two weeks, she explained, hiking one hundred miles in all. She had her clothes packed, but when they got there, her parents changed the plan. Esther would drive back to St. Maries with my mother. My mother's older sister, Barbara, twenty-three and visiting home from college, would go with George alone.

Growing up, we visited Aunt Barbara maybe once a year. She died of breast cancer when I was in my early thirties. I remember a woman daintily beautiful, with dark hair and narrow, fine-boned shoulders. She was unbelievably kind. I never heard a cross word from her. She also had a royal air to her that made her seem distant, irreproachable. When I saw the two sisters side-by-side, looking almost like twins though they were ten years apart, I could appreciate my mother's quirks and vulnerabilities, her dark moods and fierceness.

"I'll never forget how Mother rubbed Barbara's hands and then took my wool mittens and put them on her and kissed her on the neck," my mother continued, eyes fixed like plastic buttons on the parking lot buzzing with men and women in wrinkled clothes, haggard and weary after a day's work. "I just stood back watching Barbara soaking up the attention, aware I was being left out."

The reversal had been traumatic for my mother, to be shut out of the wilderness so suddenly and without explanation, and because she didn't understand it, I was filled with tenderness for her. My mother said she could still see it as if it were yesterday, her father and Barbara turning their backs and ambling into the woods with their Trapper Nelson packs filled with tea, bread, and dried meat. I could see them, too, George and Barbara, not actual people but cloudy, dreamy figures, taking something deep and primal from my mother, something I sensed in her clearly roiling emotion as she told the story. My mother didn't have tears in her eyes, but in another time and place, she might have.

Throughout my childhood, anything could move her to tears. A woman at a park yelling at her child, the abuse of the powerless. Television news footage of soldiers returning from Vietnam in body bags, the violence, the waste of young lives. A neighbor driving a new car, driving home our disadvantages—we had only bicycles for transportation. Sometimes nothing in the outside world. Until I started school and glimpsed other families, I thought every mother in the world cried on a daily basis. It was all I knew.

I also knew that once my mother pulled herself together after a cry, there was a period of quietness followed by great activity. She'd take us to the park to fly kites or the arboretum to name plants or to the beach to hunt for shells, and while these adventures had a lovely carefree charm, I was on edge because I didn't know when she might break down again. It was the quietness I liked the most, a curtain between two realities. I can still feel my brothers and me cuddled on the couch in a tumble of arms and legs as we listened to her read a novel or poem, the time sweet against the moments of anguish and action.

My brothers soothed my mother. They formed a pillar of calm with their intuitive ways of caring about her, a hand on her shoulder, a nod, or asking something simple—could she reach the cereal in the high cupboard?—that she could fulfill instantly. I was difficult, demanding. It seemed the warmth of her love shone on them instead of me. Rather than resenting my brothers, I adored them as she did. When she lavished praise or took them on special outings without me, they didn't seem rivals as much as conduits through which I could experience her love.

When I reached my teens, I tried to figure out what caused the routine sobbing. I wondered if my mother was just hungry. She was forever dieting, reading labels, concocting low-calorie high-nutrition recipes on what little money we had. She eventually went to work for the diet chain Weight Watchers. Over time I believed her sorrow came from a different kind of hunger—she was starved for affection. Although she and my grandmother had intimate conversations during our vacations in Idaho, Esther's daily phone calls put my mother on edge. After she hung up, my mother would wail, "I can't do anything to please her," forehead in hands. My brothers and I gathered round the dining room table, addicted to the depth of her feeling. Because I seemed to please my grandmother without even trying, I felt pitted against my mother, responsible for her hurt. Though not so responsible that I was willing to give up Esther.

Sometimes my mother's crying made me curious—I was attracted to its mystery—and sometimes anxious, and I'd flee to my room with an ache in my gut. The effects of the crying spilled into my nights, and when I suffered insomnia and nightmares, I'd whine for my mother to stretch out at the foot of my bed until I drifted off. She obliged though she was dead tired from all she did for us—for me. Why didn't I consider the laundry and cooking, cleaning and shopping, carrying me to gymnastics and piano lessons, lonely days surrounded by children? Part of me wonders if anything would be different today if I had.

But in the Safeway parking lot, though she was clearly upset, I felt us growing close without tears, without brothers. "It was too late for Mother and me to drive back home," my mother said. "So we stayed at the Lost Horse Trailhead that night." They needed protection from frost and bears and cougars. "We crawled under the 1950 Dodge and pulled a thin blanket over ourselves," she said. "Imagine that."

"How'd you fit?"

"Cars were a lot higher back then."

She lay there, she said, eyes wide open, shivering, thinking about her sister and father drifting deeper into the woods as she drifted into sleep.

When she woke in the morning, Esther was gone, her blanket frozen to the ice, and there was no trace of her.

All I could think was how my mother was left in the dark under a cold car without her mother, how desolate she must have felt, how bereft, and there we were, snugged in my warm car, evening sun pouring through the windows. It made my stomach clench.

"I was just a kid and all alone," she said. "Mom had never vanished like that, so I probably was worried. But I've never been one to panic. And," her eyes brightened and she buckled her lip in a smirk, "I could drive at fourteen, my dad had taught me, and the keys were still in the car." She said she tried to track Esther, but the ground was hard and there were no prints. "I think I built a fire, and I sang to myself. But something happened during those hours on the edge of the wilderness," she said. "A kind of inner fire lit up inside me, and I understood that I could take care of myself no matter what."

"Where'd Grandma go?" I asked.

"I don't know," she said in a voice like a thin string she plucked with longing. "Sometime that afternoon, she was just there. I didn't see her come out of the forest, but she must have—there was nowhere else. I don't know if she was searching for Dad and Barbara, if she was as disappointed as I was at not being able to go, or if she just wandered off. I must have asked her where she went. I must have. Of course, she never liked to talk about disturbing things."

I wasn't sure what I was hearing. Esther, my totem figure. My idol. Her death had knocked me flat. I felt her absence in the backs of my knees, the undersides of my elbows, my armpits, and my groin, places where the skin is thin and the veins close to the surface. In some ways, she wasn't absent at all. She lived on in my dreams, appearing on the edges or as a major character, guiding me or scolding me or warning me. But there in the car, that character took on a new dimension. How could she leave my mother alone like that? How could she not have explained her disappearance?

Lost Horse seemed a world away then, and though I didn't yet know how I would get there, I understood I would eventually go, following a path to the center of something secret about my mother, my grandparents, myself. Now, standing at the trailhead, I took a long breath, exhaling doubt into the soft air, snapped together my waist buckle, and started down the path behind Myron and my father. We padded along, not talking, keeping pace with our own breath, huge packs riding our hips.

5 Life That Thrives

October 15, 2018

Connie's disappearance has me stumbling through the next week teaching my classes at the university, meeting students, attending committee meetings. I spend numb days and blind nights staring into the abyss of social media where people summon her from wherever she is.

"She may have taken a long jaunt and still be out there waiting to be rescued," someone speculates on October 11.

Honestly, we don't know.

By October 15, hope dwindles. Twelve days alone in the wilderness. One person writes: "She was a little Pixie Faery one moment and Wonder Woman the next. If people worried about her age, they shouldn't, she'd made over seventy free falls—a maneuver done by smokejumpers—and was planning a new one in the following spring." Someone remembers how back in 1988, she'd wanted to jump out of a plane during a homecoming game and land on the fifty-yard line for a coin toss. Someone else recalls how she would run down the hall in the Forest Service station in high heels, how she loved switching from heels to hiking boots. Another notes that she taught at Lapwai on Nimíipuu homeland, had many friends there, and shared her stories of horses and mules. They call her a ray of sunshine.

Though later I will learn that she rode with a mule pack string the seventeen miles from Moose Creek Ranger Station to the hunting camp at a place called Big Rock, someone writes that she hiked it, and I cling to this idea. Hiking alone. Not unusual for her. She told me herself once, "I know the trails, and I know the routes and where you could cross in high water, I know the stopping places and how to get out of a dangerous spot." For twenty-five years, one of her jobs was visitor contacts—she hated bureaucratic words—which she referred to simply as teaching. She educated people on why certain rules are there, why you scattered your fire ring before you left a campsite—leave no trace ethics—had no shame in instructing some old mountain man to dig a one-foot cat hole to bury his poop. She called it part philosophy, part actual, physical use of the wilderness. She knew the terrain, knew the people. "Every teacher knows that you approach each audience differently," she told me. "You deal with a backpacker differently than a cowboy."

By all accounts, Connie arrived at the Big Rock hunting camp in fine shape, unpacked, and set up her kit. The hunters left her the next morning for a different hunting ground. They would be back. Connie preferred to be alone in the woods anyway.

People add to social media daily. They tell about the rescue effort. Firefighters and smokejumpers, FLIR heat technology, the US Air Force and the Idaho National Guard, backcountry horsemen and volunteers from the Selway-Bitterroot Frank Church Foundation, and local search and rescue groups with helicopters and canine units. People climbing vertical rock faces and crawling on their bellies for a mile under thick brush. The Idaho County Sheriff's office. Friends from near and far. Connie knew everyone. So many people saw her as a friend, a mentor, a sister, a mother figure. She adopted people, and they adopted her.

I scroll and scroll, but one thought grips me: I have to go there.

6 Vision

A memory: Esther's St. Maries living room, stretched squares of aquamarine, ruby, and topaz falling through the window and through me. This is my earliest recollection and my most persistent, the one that chases me down when I'm squeezing avocados at the grocery store, staring at a traffic light through rain-soaked windows, sitting in the gray space of a faculty meeting, the memory that hovers on the edge of sleep.

Mother and Grandmother are there. The house is quiet, no fighting noises from brothers, no booming explanations from Father. Mother and Grandmother, usually in jeans and sweatshirts, are dressed up. In memory, I see velvet sleeves, mink or marten collars, felt hats, dark stockings, tulle hemlines, polished shoes, black gloves. I'm enchanted; I'm in love.

Mother and Grandmother are sitting in chairs across from one another. Mother is young and smooth, no sharp edges on her face or body, but there are edges in the room, invisible tensions slicing the air.

I can't tell if I'm sitting on the floor between them or suspended

George Washington Case, 1930. Family photo.

in the corner as in a dream. I don't know how old I am, recall nothing before or after. This event stands alone, solitary, like a distant planet.

Mother is clearer than Grandmother, whose face I can't make out. I can only feel the heavy eyes, the soft neck, the stiff mouth. Both of their heads are bent. They're crying. Maybe they have tissues.

The light heightens. I'm afraid.

⟡

This vision followed me throughout my childhood and young adulthood, and then, when I was in my late twenties, when my own daughter, Steph, was born, I attached an event to it: George's funeral.

I knew nothing about his funeral, where it was held, who attended, whether he was buried or cremated, or how anyone in the family felt about it. I never heard about it from anyone, not even tiny snippets while I was growing up. But I somehow believed that this vision was connected to his death.

When I was in my late thirties, I narrated the dreamlike memory to my mother in her kitchen, convinced that she would validate it. "No," she said, abruptly, pulling plates from the dishwasher and clicking them into the cupboard, "that never happened."

"So, I'm just making this up?" I snapped. "This thing I've remembered all my life?"

"I don't know, but it didn't happen."

I bristled. There'd been other times when our versions of events clashed. Like the day she misplaced one of my brothers. I was all of six years old. We were at a grocery store and had returned to our car when my mother said, "Where's Michael?" referring to the two-year-old. I remembered her hair was tied back in a thick pony and her eyes squinted behind heavy cat-eye glasses as she screamed panicked sounds, barely words, telling me to hang on to the grocery cart while Esther, who happened to be visiting, held the other brother. I fought to steady the metal basket, confused, searching for some reassurance on my grandmother's face but finding only the nervous twitch of her lips. It wasn't long before my mother came back carrying the toddler and laughing—yes, laughing. She'd been striding the aisles, she said through attempts at catching her breath, calling his name, when she realized he was right there on her hip. "I was carrying him all along!" she said, her voice shining.

I had replayed the scene over the years, adding layers of meaning, until the memory became a parable. Neither I nor my grandmother noticed my brother on my mother's hip before she ran back into the store—why? For a long time I thought my mother's terror had so saturated the moment that we accepted her version of reality. She was like that, my mother— powerful. Later, I believed the story showed how she and my brothers were joined at the hip, so much so that their connection went unnoticed, how all of us children were bone of her bone. The hip, the pelvis, the body's meeting place, the center of life, holding together the spine and the legs, the heart and the feet. That was my mother, too. Still later, I came to think of the lost brother as an artistic awakening. Because as my mother ran back into the store, I wasn't actually worried about her and my brother as much as mesmerized by the slow unfolding of the moment. It was the first time I felt life turn to story as it was happening and understood the power I had in shaping the narrative.

I harnessed that power the day I sat in her kitchen describing my earliest recollection. Her insistence that my memory of my grandmother and her crying together was false only made me believe in it more. After that, I found myself adding threads of story. I could see my mother's dress in royal violet boiled wool, her glossy dark hair falling down her face like a veil, and my grandmother's lace slip falling beneath her black crepe shift, her face red and puffy from tears. I felt the memory as something whole, a shimmering vision that tied me to these two women through tears, through death, as if the essence of us arose from that moment.

Whether the two most important women in my life crying together in a jewel-colored vision was real or imaginary or a little bit of both, I'll never know. In any case, it's notable that George was at the center, the invisible bond holding us together.

7 Box

What seems like a vision but is absolutely real is the day I visited Esther in the St. Maries Care Center. It was a snowy day in February 1999, a week after she'd had the stroke that would kill her.

Made of corrugated metal, the care center sits on the outskirts of town. Fifty years earlier, when my mother was a teenager, loggers and miners had clogged the streets, and logging and mining were still in operation, though somewhat diminished from their former glory, the summer I spent with Esther when I was sixteen. Now neither industry flourished. The boarded windows and For Rent signs along Main Street stirred a sense of loss in my core. St. Maries was a place receding into the past and might one day be a ghost town.

State Hospital North laundry building ironing room, Orofino, Idaho. No date.
ITD Headquarters Collection. Courtesy of Idaho State Archives.

"They've got me in a torture chamber," my grandmother said when I arrived, her words garbled. She was sitting in a wheelchair next to a plastic fountain, water splashing with a pang in the shallow fabricated basin, accentuating the loneliness of the room, where not another soul was in sight. My grandmother's hair was curled too tightly to her scalp, her eyes too large for her head, her rigid mouth had gone slack, a new sign of vulnerability, and I felt all trembly just standing in her presence.

"Torture chamber?" I studied the walls lined with watercolors of baby animals and children. Then I remembered her aversion to doctors and hospitals, how in her ninety-one years on this Earth, she never willingly entered a medical facility, never had a flu shot or took an antibiotic or pain killer, never got a physical, mammogram, colonoscopy, or any number of tests recommended for the aging. She lived by her own folk medicine, part mysticism, pieced together from various religious thought, and part herbal concoctions from her garden. She used to talk to her plants as if they were companions. She must have missed them in this place.

I hugged her and accompanied her to physical therapy. Laid flat on a table like a corpse, she couldn't move much, but she tried to communicate. "You know, I've walked up so many mountains," she told the therapist, a young man with stringy brown hair in a ponytail. Her legs were long and bony, and I was a little shocked at how white her skin was. The therapist bent one leg and then the other, trying, he said, to rewire her brain.

Afterward, I wheeled her around the center and we stopped back at the plastic fountain. "This isn't a bad place," I said, mostly just to say something. "Who else has been to visit, besides Mom?"

"An old preacher came and blew his bad breath in my face yesterday." She chuckled. "But he meant well."

That was my grandmother, irreverent to the end.

She was silent for a moment and then, apropos of nothing, she said, "I didn't do right by your mother," in a voice thin as parchment. She turned her head and looked away. "I'm nuts," I heard her say. Something in me militated against the claim, and I said, "No, you're not nuts, Grandma," even as my mother's voice echoed in my mind: "Grandma went through a rough period when her mind wasn't right."

I don't recall when my mother first said these words to me, where we were or how old I was—my early twenties, probably. But I remember her eyes were large and glassy as she told me about the mental ward where George took Esther when my mother was fourteen. My mother's tone was flat and bland, but the way she looked at me, I knew she was communicating something private and delicate about the family, about herself. Still, I denied it. I could not picture my grandmother in a mental ward, and yet I felt a bright sting, sensed something big and scary and inevitable behind the phrase *her mind wasn't right*, an arc stretching from Esther to my mother to me and possibly my future children—maybe a daughter, maybe a granddaughter. A constellation swaying into chaos, off-kilter, disordered. After that, my mother mentioned Esther's mental illness once in a while, but never in enough detail for me to understand what had ailed her. I never broached the subject with my grandmother, too afraid speaking it might bring it into being. I wish I could say I asked her to explain that day in the care center, let her speak her own story, but I didn't. Instead, I clung to the strange entanglement I'd lived with for some time: the story of the mental hospital, my disbelief, and my gnawing sense that it might be true.

I wheeled her back to her room, helped her into bed.

"I want you to go to my house," she said. "The key is on the ledge above the doorjamb."

I stroked her bony shoulder, and through my strokes, I was telling her not to make me leave.

"I've always loved you," she whispered. "But I'm at the end of my life."

When she said this, something zapped inside of me. No, she couldn't be. She would get better. No, I would not accept it. When I look back, I realize she was slipping from this world—I saw her frailty, her pain, her immobile legs and too-large eyes, heard her thin voice deformed by the stroke, but at the time, I couldn't imagine her gone.

The last thing she said was, "Go. Take the box."

What did she mean by *the box*? I didn't want to ask, didn't want to drain her energy. I sat with her until she fell asleep. If I'd have known I'd never see her again, I wouldn't have left. But I didn't know, so I drove the icy roads to her house as evening fell.

Inside, everything was familiar: dark linoleum floors, rickety furniture, and the ripe, gray odor of secondhand clothes bound for the thrift store. It occurred to me that my mother would not want me in there without permission, yet Esther had told me to come. Was I an incompetent thief or just obeying orders? I searched the shelves for the photo album I'd seen when I was sixteen. Gone. My throat grew tight, thinking my mother had taken it.

But then I spotted Esther's beloved Mary Baker Eddy volumes. She'd underlined a passage—"Man is the generic term for all humanity. Woman is the highest species of man"—and written *YES*. I smiled, remembering how she'd refused to pay taxes for the last ten years of her life, because, as she claimed, "I've paid enough," how she refused other things, to remarry, to wear a dress or skirt, to wear lipstick, to wear a polite attitude. But this was the first evidence I'd seen of a blatantly feminist stance, and an eerie feeling that everything was as it should be snuck up on me and then vanished.

She'd marked other passages. "Spirit and its formations are the only realities." Her guiding principle. Every person, animal, plant, rock, and body of water—everything on Earth had a spirit life more real than the matter we could see in front of our faces. The afterlife, too, was no static place but a zone in which spirits continued to evolve. My own spiritual beliefs were strong but not as well formed as my grandmother's. Still, I felt kinship with her sense of the afterlife that evening.

I climbed to the attic. The 16 mm films were gone, too. Unsettled, increasingly suspicious that my mother had tampered with the only evidence of Esther's life before I could remember, I headed back to the living room. It was then I noticed a rectangular cardboard box on her one piece of good furniture, a sideboard. Heavily scratched and stained, the box was the size of a small briefcase. Peculiar. When I was a child, Esther's house was filled with odd and curious objects. Through the years, she'd given away or hauled to the thrift store almost everything. She owned so few possessions it was impossible to miss what she did have. I had never seen this box.

I cracked open the lid as if peeking into her mind: papers, letters, a diary, and news clippings. A photo of a man I would later recognize as my grandfather climbing out of a snow hole. Another of a log building, and on the back Esther's slanted handwriting: "Moose Creek Ranger

Station, in the Selway-Bitterroot Wilderness, where I spent many miserable years married to a man I didn't love and who didn't love me." The words fell off the picture and splattered onto the floor. Although Myron and I had married young, our years together had felt like a true partnership, anything but miserable. Who was this man, my grandfather? What kind of prison was Moose Creek Ranger Station?

Delving further into the box's depths felt impossible in the fading light. As a literary historian, I knew if I kept prying, I'd feel compelled to examine everything with an archivist's eye. And Esther's words on the photograph had made me fearful of the contents in the way you can be frightened of what you most desire. The box was a message in a bottle, a lifetime of bottled-up memories and feelings, a beautiful evil, the curse of Pandora, meant to stay shut for the time being.

Go. Take the box.

I replaced the lid, set the box in the trunk of my car, and drove home.

8 Station

The backpacking trek with Myron and my father from Lost Horse to Moose Creek Ranger Station took place some fourteen years ago. I've lost many of the specifics but I vividly remember that the trip didn't start out well. I would not have believed it if I hadn't seen it with my own eyes. A ghost forest. Dead trees by the thousands through a valley and up hillsides, what seemed to me then to be a war zone stretching for miles. Some trees stood. Some were crumbling charcoal. Hundreds lay across the landscape, fallen soldiers.

The horror of that dead valley may not have seemed so all consuming if not for the fact that we'd spent a pleasant first day of backpacking.

Moose Creek Ranger Station, 1925. Family photo.

Our campsite that first night was nestled in a stand of trees, sweet and protected. A calm settled over me and a curiosity about the place beyond George and Esther and her *many miserable years.* At dawn, we gulped coffee, and whatever I expected going forward, I certainly didn't anticipate a ghost forest.

"Old fire," Myron said as we stood in the valley in the mid-morning sun. He removed his cap and wiped his brow, his hair falling in ropey, sweat-soaked strands. The dead lodgepoles, which seemed to me ragged arms reaching for a past, were crowded by thousands of young trees my height or shorter, glowing bright green. A charred smell blended with a peppery scent in the soft light of midmorning.

"The trail crew must have missed this patch," my father said as we climbed over the first tree lying across the trail. A few yards later, we came to another, larger in diameter. My father, who is six feet tall, and Myron at six-one, hopped up, sat down, swung both feet over, and used poles to brace themselves as they landed. I was too short for that maneuver. I threw one leg over, hugging the trunk as one would a lover, and fell to the other side, painfully slamming into the ground with the full weight of my pack.

I straddled another blowdown, and another and another within a few hundred yards, and just as I was getting a rhythm, my bare thigh caught on a broken branch. A hot sting, then deep pain in my groin and general throbbing as blood ran down my leg. I wiped the blood with my hand, which dried quickly in the heat, and my mind fogged with confusion as I glanced up at the massive valley and the sides of two mountains covered in silver snags. A sense of devastation overcame me. What had possessed me to come here?

Ahead of me, Myron was moving in smooth advances and pauses, swinging his body over giant trunks with ease. I had no choice but to keep going, and I did, until Myron stopped to let me catch up. "Let me take your pack," he said. I mindlessly unbuckled it and, as he lifted it from my shoulders, I levitated several feet off the ground. He shoved a water bottle in my hand, and I drank.

"More," he said.

I slid back into my pack and, still floating, seemed to arrive immediately at the next blowdown. I hoisted myself over, catching a shin and ripping the flesh, but instead of wiping the blood, I shuffled forward. It would dry into a scab before I could reach for a Band-Aid, anyway. Myron was immediately on my shoulder handing me water.

"I'm fine," I snapped, unsure why I was so testy with him, which only added to my unease. Myron and I had met on a stark farming landscape as eighteen-year-olds at a small, religious co-op school in Saskatchewan, a school Esther had found for me and paid for. The first time I saw him, he was playing catch. "You remind me of my brothers," I yelled from the field's edge, which turned out to be a premonition. We'd been together so long, sometimes we seemed to be part of the same family, or extensions of one another, but there in the wilderness, I felt a gaping distance between us, and it scared me. At the same time, a strange independence was taking over. The landscape became very small, and a weary confidence rose in me. I could do this. I could. I would. And I would do it alone.

Hours passed as we made our way through the burn, running on adrenaline, desperation, heat, and nerves. Just as the sun dipped below the mountain peaks, we entered the shade of an old-growth forest, moss hanging from trees like shrouds. The temperature dropped ten degrees, the spicy scents of vegetation flooded the air, and the tensions that had built through the afternoon like a thundercloud loosened. Myron and my father tramped ahead, and soon I couldn't see them, so I walked on for several miles until I heard water. Yes, Jeannette Creek. My father had said we would camp at Jeannette Creek. When I reached the sound, though, I saw a chute of huge, angular boulders over which a torrent of water boomed, gathering in foaming pools and running on in a series of broken rapids. We wouldn't be able to make camp because there was not one square foot of flat ground.

Myron, pack, shirt, sunglasses, and ball cap tossed on the bank, was sitting on a boulder, his thick brown hair wet. He pushed the hair from his eyes and said, with a kind of glee in his voice, "I didn't know this place would be so rugged." How could he be smiling? Pain pulsed through my veins and sweat poured into the gully of my back. I discovered blood from my various wounds had rusted down my arms and legs. The pinch of confidence I'd felt earlier vanished, and fatigue beyond thought came to me. Myron jumped from the rock and asked if I was okay. I brushed him away and said I could take care of myself. His sympathy made me feel how pathetic I was. He looked stricken, and I knew in the moment I should apologize, but to admit defeat or regret of any kind would have done me in.

"Let's rest here," my father said, trying not to stare at me. Instantly my knees gave out, and I sank down on the bank. My father and Myron dug into their packs while I removed my boots and socks to find my feet bloody, too. Blisters had formed, some full of pus, others ripped and red. I thrust my feet in the icy water until they went numb. Wretched place, I thought. I despised it and desired it, an ambivalence close to how I felt about the box my grandmother had bequeathed to me on her deathbed.

I had opened the box a few months earlier on my front porch, alone in the late spring light, moist green in the air. I held paper and pen to make a record of the contents, proper archivist that I am, but also as a way to steady my nerves. I lifted the lid. From the top, I took out twelve black-and-white photographs—all of George. Dark hair; a small, angular build; and narrow piercing eyes, like the face I remembered from Esther's album. Most were taken in the Bitterroots. In one, he stood crotch-deep in snow bending down to touch a young elk. In others he was with other men in the forest. There was also, as I remembered from my first peek into the box, the photo with Esther's caption regarding the *many miserable years*.

Next, Esther's diary. A cheap drugstore variety covered in a floral pattern, in which she recorded romances and potential ones: *Jan 3, 1984, Had a letter and a phone call from Red Whittaker at Big Fork, Montana. He sounded real nice over the phone—Now to decide whether to pursue the acquaintance or not??* I placed the photo of the *many miserable years* next to the diary. Maybe misery released passion later in life, allowed her to revive old friendships and pursue love interests.

Otherwise, the collage-like structure, bright fragments from daily activities juxtaposed with passages of despair, most struck me: *Feb 11, Am getting the walnuts all shelled. Stopped at the Thrift Store. Only 3 people there. Didn't sleep good last night. Existence is futile anymore.* I could see her mood shifting right there on the page, trying on provisional identities, revealing an intimate part of herself, then regretting it. She had scratched some pages so heavily, the pen had actually torn the paper.

I set the diary aside and unpacked dozens of condolence cards with envelopes from Ohio, California, Washington, Montana, Kansas,

addressed to Esther after George died from a bleeding ulcer with compli-
cations from alcoholism in 1962. "I can't hardly believe it," one said, and
I felt the suddenness of his passing, how she was left alone in a moment,
even if she didn't love him.

Underneath the cards were newspaper clippings about David Miles. I
had not thought about David in years, but I could still hear his baritone
voice and see his thick silver hair. I knew from what my grandmother
had told me that she and her sister Hattie had been friendly with several prominent Nimíipuu families from Sweetwater and Kooskia, including David, a tribal elder. My grandmother and David had attended high
school in Kooskia and college at Lewiston Normal School together, and
their friendship had lasted.

When I reached the bottom of the box, I stopped. I couldn't believe it.
I pulled out a book titled *Memoirs*. I rifled through the manuscript of fifty-
six pages, trying not to get my hopes up. I wanted revelations, answers,
though what kind of answers was still unclear to me. What I read were
childhood stories. Profiles of Esther's twelve sisters and brothers. Songs
and poems she'd copied out. Sketches she'd made of the ridge where she'd
grown up above the Clearwater River. And then, my hands trembled a
little as I opened to a section called "Wilderness Living" and read about
the first time she'd come to Moose Creek:

> The Selway River trail to Moose Creek Ranger Station took off
> from Selway Falls winding over bluffs, down to creek bottoms, and
> up over hills. Much of it is rocky. My first trip to Moose Creek
> was in the spring of 1930 on a beautiful young mare named Toddy.
> We mounted our horses that first morning for a fifteen mile ride
> to Three Links packer cabin. But the trail near Cupboard Creek
> wound over the top of a cliff hundreds of feet high. Being of a
> timid nature I would dismount and lead my horse around the
> places where the trail was narrow.

A world far away and back in time. Esther's connection to the land
lived in those pages. Though she'd grown up on the edge of the Bitterroot Mountains, she arrived in the middle of the wilderness sight
unseen after the wedding. I read about how lonely she felt, but was she

afraid? She called herself timid, but within a short time, she had a rough love for the trail. "I didn't stay at the station much as every chance I got I rode the trails with George," she wrote. I saw her relaxing into the land, saw a foot in a stirrup, a leg thrown over the animal's back, swaying with its body as it clomped along, dodging tree branches, wiping sweat off her forehead, young, alive. What had happened to make her hate her life there, to turn away and never return? Nothing of that could be found in the *Memoirs*, even between the lines. Still, a sickening feeling for George welled up. *Many miserable years*. What had he done to her? Her gift of the box seemed to be asking me to find out, just as the wilderness itself was pushing me on.

The ghost forest where I now sat, treacherous and seemingly endless, reflected the obstacles between what I knew about my grandparents and what I needed to know, and somehow, even with blistered feet, legs cross-hatched with welts and scabs that would turn to scars I would wear for the rest of my life, I could not turn back. While I bandaged my feet and slipped them into my boots, I could hear Myron and my father talking above the crashing water.

"Are we going to have to carry her out?" my father was saying in genuine concern.

"I've never seen her like this," Myron said. "She won't let me help." Though he sounded macho and a little aggrieved, he respected me and my need to go forward on my own.

My father said he would walk ahead, locate a campsite, and return to get us.

"I just can't tell where we'll find one," Myron said. "It might be miles."

I kept my eyes on the water. I couldn't let them know I was listening, but I heard what they were really saying—I should rise and walk. I stood and they came to me, Myron holding my pack, helping me glide into the straps, and my father looking at me with his aquiline nose and goofy snaggle-toothed smile, which suddenly made me laugh. After that, we tramped mindlessly like zombies or sleepwalkers for several miles until we came to a sheer overhang of sparkling gray granite, the only flat place we'd seen. Jeanette Mountain's peeling face rose one thousand feet in front of us.

"This'll have to do," my father said, dropping his pack. He moved slowly along the overhang and peered into the gorge below. Myron darted about, reaching, kneeling, jumping up, pulling out the tent, and hunting for rocks to use instead of stakes. Where did he get his energy? I pulled off my boots and limped over to a creek, scrubbing off the grime and dried blood, and quiet washed over me. Endorphins.

After a dinner of freeze-dried noodles and trail mix, my father knelt on the rock, maps spread around him. Now that the sun had set, his shadowed eyes appeared lined with exhaustion. "Only eight miles to our next camp spot," he said, calmly. Calculating mileage seemed to quell his anxiety.

"I've never been this far from civilization," I said. "We could die out here, and no one would know." I didn't say more, but as I turned the thought over in my mind, I found it strangely soothing.

"Connie's expecting us at Moose Creek," Myron said. "We won't be missed too long."

I tried to imagine the station. I had my grandmother's description from her *Memoirs*: "a large log house with four back rooms finished into a kitchen, dining room, office, and bedroom. Rough board floors whip-sawed out of logs and holes cut for doors and windows. Mantys, 10 x 10 foot canvas covers used as packing material for movement by horse-back, were hung at the doors and windows. One of these rooms was our bed-room." It sounded romantic, but all I could see was the unhappy marriage and a faceless woman named Connie through the cloud of Joe's hero worship. Connie. The woman ranger I had to ask about history.

✧

I saw the station for the first time five days later on a bright afternoon. My feet had healed, more or less, and those feet took off ahead of Myron and my father.

The station compound is made up of twelve log structures built from local materials—fir trees, hand-split cedar shakes, and native granite. It sits at the apex of two grassy airfields that cross one another to form an X. The structures and airfields stretch across a raised plateau the shape of a giant pelvis, which drops in steep canyons on each side. Down one canyon flows the Selway River; down the other runs Moose Creek, more a river than a creek. At the end of the plateau, the two waters join and the Selway almost doubles in size.

The twelve log buildings at the ranger station stand in a patchwork pattern, laid out like a little town. As I walked toward it, I could feel that I was at the center of something important to other people at least as much as it was to me. A water faucet fed by a spring, a corral, a barn, other buildings. Each displayed a sign indicating the date when it was built. There wasn't a soul in sight. The place looked like a ghost town.

I dropped my pack at 1933, the ranger's dwelling, where Esther and George had lived. An onslaught of grasshoppers, curious spring-wound legs and weird eyeballs, followed as I tramped around. I tried the door. Locked. So this was the site of Esther's conflict, the place from which she rode the trails and then traveled to a deep unhappiness, a ghost forest of her mind.

All this time, it had been impossible to picture her in the wilderness as a woman of twenty-six, having left her job as a nanny in Lewiston to marry George. As a young woman, she was close to her twelve brothers and sisters, and even when I knew her, she was a real homebody, tending her garden, working at the thrift store, playing cards at the senior center; no wonder she felt isolated. But how could she be unhappy surrounded by millions of acres of trees and mountains and rivers?

One of these rooms was our bedroom.

I circled the dwelling, trying each window. Maybe I could crawl through, but each was locked, and at the last one, a sign nailed to the outside wall read: "Property of the United States. All persons are prohibited under penalty of the law from committing trespass."

I walked over to the main station, a few yards away. A man in slacks, with delicate hands and a bald forehead shaped like a triangle, told me he was the volunteer ranger.

"Is Connie here?" I asked.

"No," he said, brushing a woven, wide-brimmed hat against his thigh. "She's out on trails and won't be back for weeks." He said he hadn't even met her, and he left.

I knelt down by the bright yellow sign, rusted with age. *Prohibited under penalty of law.*

When I recollect that sign today, I think immediately of Connie. It would be another year before I would meet her, and many more before I understood the nuances of Moose Creek Ranger Station or her words in the Moose Creek logbook:

> When one is attached to a place and feels ownership, not deserved but seized, it is difficult to leave and put it in the hands of someone else. Surely no one could love and care for it as we do. Still, a long time ago, Moose Creekers claimed they knew the right way, cared the most, did it best. To return to a Moose Creek that is alive and well and very much loved is satisfying, almost overwhelming.

I see now that Connie was referring to something bigger than wilderness. None of us really owns the Earth, she was saying, even if we can wave titles to houses or high-rises or acreages for the short duration of our lives. This is a lesson I relearn again and again. Even today it's impossible for me to visit the wilderness and not feel a tinge of possessiveness. But on that first glimpse, I felt the overwhelming seize of ownership, felt the dwelling, the station, the airfield, were my birthright. My inheritance. I took the Prohibited sign as an affront, but even so, I sensed its deeper meaning. I couldn't get attached to this land.

And yet, as if Esther had planned it, I already had.

9 Glacier Lilies

Shortly after Esther died in 1999, I summoned the courage to ask my mother about the photo album I'd seen in St. Maries the summer I lived with her. I don't recall where we were, only my mother's emphatic, "I don't have it!"

I was convinced she did, that it was stowed away in the basement or under the stairs, that she was keeping it from me on purpose. But when I pressed my mother, she shrugged. "I think Mom burned the photos."

I asked why she would do such a thing.

"I don't know," she said casually. "They haunted her."

Dick Walker on Moose Creek airstrip, 2019. Nick Gerhardt photo. Courtesy of Dick Walker.

Haunted. Such a loaded word, as if the dead lived in those images, outside of time. I kept asking why. My mother kept saying, "I don't know."

I lived with the uncertainty over the whereabouts of those photos for years, gradually accepting my mother's story of the lost images and even adding to that story—Esther had destroyed all vestiges of her youth and life at Moose Creek because she was not just haunted, but tormented, tortured, by what they contained. Childhood poverty with a depressed father and a shadowy mother on a ridge near the wilderness. Marriage to a wild man wrapped in a bearskin or crawling out of a snow hole. And then the story I'd created abruptly changed.

Some months after I beheld Moose Creek Ranger Station and the Prohibited sign for the first time, I drove to the small town of Grangeville, Idaho, two and a half hours southeast of my house in Moscow. It was a warm spring day, the trillium, buttercup, and fairy slipper bursting out of the ditches along the highway. I pulled up to a one-story, bungalow-style Forest Service building. Inside, a woman wearing a khaki uniform with a gold name badge (Cindy | Archeologist | Nez Perce National Forest), met me and showed me through a locked door where other men and women in jeans and fleece vests bustled around. Cindy kept her head bowed and didn't smile.

"Sorry to take up your time," I said. I thought I sensed her annoyance.

"That's okay." Her voice was velvety, almost convincing.

Cindy looked to be the same age (mid-forties) and the same height (five feet two) as me. And she had information I wanted. I had contacted her asking if she had any materials relating to my grandparents in the wilderness. Yes, she had said, and she invited me to visit. I'd cleaned my car to make room for boxes I assumed I'd be hauling back. But now, at her cubicle, she scooped up a surprisingly thin sheaf of papers, knocked them against the desk to straighten them, then fastened the corner with a small binder clip. "Here," she said.

I flipped through and found a grazing report from 1925 authored by my grandfather; a booklet about early pack animals and muleskinners authored by Cindy herself; and the original homestead applications of a handful of people—including George—who made the Selway-Bitterroot Wilderness their homes in the early 1900s.

"What's in those?" I tipped my head toward a wall of beige file cabinets, hoping for at least one box of papers I could burrow into over weeks. I liked nothing better than piecing together the past from old documents, fragments, and ephemera—sibylline leaves.

She pointed to the packet. "This is it." I felt mildly disappointed, and I didn't quite believe it. If George had been a homesteader and wilderness ranger for twenty-odd years, there had to be more. I told her about Esther's *Memoirs*, the one passage that troubled me above all others. Esther had written, "The last summer I left Moose Creek Ranger Station, 1942, I had the overwhelming desire to winter there. It must have been a premonition, because I never did return."

"I feel like I'm the one destined to return." I handed her my card. "If you run across anything else, I'd love to know about it."

Cindy took it with a placid expression. "I lived at Moose Creek in the seventies when my dad was ranger," she said. "Pretty special place."

She rested her hands on her intricate cowboy belt buckle. "You should contact Dick Walker. He lives in the mountains above Peck." Dick Walker, she said, knew more about Bitterroot history than anyone. Some people called him Mr. Selway. "He has a bunch of documents and photos, but he's protective." I asked what she meant. "He doesn't give it to people and barely lets anyone see it." She jotted down Dick's contact information. "It might be different with you. You should try."

If I had known that in Dick Walker Cindy was giving me far more than a file drawer of documents, I would have wasted no time, would have called him right then, from Cindy's office. But I didn't. Back home, I couldn't bring myself to pick up the phone. I pictured myself driving up a lonely mountain road, arriving at his place, and seeing him swagger out with a loaded shotgun, crazed eyes, a rough beard, rotten teeth, and ultra-conservative rhetoric, which says a lot about my ignorance at the time. Though I was living in Idaho myself, my head was in the university, in an intellectual bubble. In my understanding of Idaho, I was in many ways still that sixteen-year-old Seattleite who'd come to Esther's St. Maries house ready to sunbathe.

It might be different with you. No, it wouldn't be different with me, I told myself. Nothing special about my wilderness experience. Over the next few weeks, though I tried to tamp down my curiosity and gnawing anticipation, Dick's name became an itch I had to scratch. The thought of all those papers and photographs and what they might contain kept me up at night. When I couldn't stand it any longer, I nervously dialed his number.

"Well, *heeeeello, ma'am*." Dick's voice unscrolled in a thick drawl after I introduced myself. I'd expected a Western outlaw and got instead the accent of a Southern gentleman.

I asked if I could pay him a visit. "From what I've heard, you embody the Selway-Bitterroot Wilderness."

On the other end of the line, I heard a *well* and a *hum* and an *ah*. Dick didn't know what his plans were for the next few weeks, and planning things didn't seem to be his strong suit. He was helping the Advocates for the West gather materials for a hearing on caribou habitat. He had a dentist appointment. He had to haul brush out of his yard. That would take half a day. He had to fix a doorknob. His dog needed shots.

"My grandparents were George and Esther Case," I said.

On the phone there was a brief pause. "Do you have a good car?" Dick asked, by which he meant a four-wheel-drive pickup.

"Yeah," I lied. I actually had a small sedan.

He barked out a list of intricate directions that involved crossing a one-lane bridge and turning at the third large pine tree on the left after a Boulder Creek Outfitters sign on a steep gravel road. I should come the next day, he said, and while I was at it, could I bring him some kale slaw from the local co-op?

When I got on the road the next morning, I had a strange sense of inevitability paired with intellectual adventure. As absurd as it seems, I felt I was meant to meet Dick, and yet I also had the sense of being led by a familiar impulse, the impulse that had sent me through libraries and archives as a scholar. But I'd never made a research trip like this one.

When I arrived an hour and a half later, Dick sauntered out of his timber-frame cabin wearing blue jeans and a flannel shirt. His graying hair was truly impressive, thick and wavy and brushed back in a Jackie O style. His eyes, the color of damp earth, narrowed as he sized me up. He was wary. I'd worn cowboy boots to impress him. He was in flip-flops.

We shook hands and, instead of inviting me in for tea, he stood on the porch telling me that if I needed to *widdle* I should go outside in the pines around his cabin. If I needed to *squat*, I was to use the composting toilet.

That was wilderness living, he said. He marched me into the bathhouse, another timber-frame building on the property, where I learned how to scoop sawdust into the toilet and start a machine that sucked noxious gas out a ceiling vent. When I think back, it seems characteristic of Dick that our introductions were uttered over a toilet—he was proud of his earthiness, unashamed of the basic functions of the body—but at the time I was nonplussed.

Inside, in Dick's kitchen, I handed him two pounds of kale slaw and a fifth of Bombay Sapphire I'd thrown in. "You want some?" he asked, holding up the bottle.

"It's ten in the morning!"

"Why not?" He poured the gin over fresh lemons and led me to a table piled with dozens of three-ring binders filled with sepia-toned photos. As I drank, he flipped through the pages, showing images of elk, moose, deer, log cabins, men on mules, and women standing in front of stoves, lives spilling out into the morning. I kept an eye out for my grandparents, but they were nowhere to be found.

He continued to turn pages, and I let the images pull me in, especially those of people I didn't recognize but felt, strangely, that I should. I placed my hand on a page where a woman was standing in front of a rickety backwoods cabin. Maybe I had seen this woman, or one like her, in the books about the early West I was reading.

"That's Mrs. Charlie Johnson," Dick said. The doorway where she stood was so small, she would have had to duck to come through it. "That's the little trapper's cabin up at Three Links Creek. It's gone now."

"She looks miserable," I said. Her dark hair was matted. She had deep, sad eyes, and wore a dirty apron.

"Her husband died back there, and she married someone else." Dick turned toward the window, a gesture I would later come to recognize as an unwillingness to speculate about a past no one could know.

"At least it gives me an idea of how my grandmother might have looked," I said. Dick turned the page. A mobile made of feathers and shells, dangling from the top lip of his windowsill, trembled, which gave me a sense of the mystery behind Dick's historic photographs, as if there was some disturbance in them, some knowing, as if the images had minds and memories of their own.

Dick made another drink, and I wandered around surveying his cabin, packed to the rafters with interesting clutter. The house served as office, photo lab, art gallery, archive, experiment in energy-efficiency housing, and—ever so sparingly—living space. Five or six desks, tucked into corners or sitting along walls, held stacks of black-and-white contact sheets, camera equipment, maps, and audiotapes. His sofas were not for sitting on but for displaying his printed, framed photos. They stood like actors waiting for an audition. There were shots of mountain peaks, bears, birds, and forests as seen from the cockpit of an airplane, matted in purples, browns, grays, and blues.

"A lot of times when I take a photograph in the wilderness, I can't help it," he said from where he was sitting at the table. "If there's something that grabs me by the short hairs, I gotta capture it. I have winter photos of white-barked pine up on Fenn Mountain. I have photos where the ptarmigan are bursting out of the snow." He waved his hands in the air, eyes wide and head cocked forward like an orchestra conductor. "They go under the snow, see. So you're skiing along, and all of a sudden, *pooooof!*"

As I would come to understand in the years that followed, Dick didn't have what most of us think of as memories. He had photos. Whenever he was talking about the past, he'd preface it by saying, "I have a photo." He rarely showed me the actual photo. Instead, he described the image to me as if it were taking place in the present.

"Hey, the glacier lilies at the bottom of the creek, they're just exploding!" Dick could change subjects on a dime.

"Those are the little yellow flowers, right?"

"Yellow with red stamens, and they pop up and droop down. Delicate and fucking beautiful."

We stepped into the sun and strolled the half mile straight down his property to Little Canyon Creek. He followed me and caught my arm now and then to make sure I didn't stumble. Pika, his blue heeler, led the way.

I learned on that ramble how Dick had spent the past thirty years collecting photographs, oral stories, and documents in preparation to write a PhD dissertation about the human history of the Selway-Bitterroot, how the PhD never came to pass, and how his two marriages didn't work out, either, though he remained friends with both women. Dick eventually turned his house, and himself, into an archive, and he found the life he was looking for.

We reached the creek and stood in the stillness until the trickling water filled our heads. Dick pointed out an ouzel's nest, and we watched the little bird whizz by in a blur.

"You know Bob Marshall?" he said.

I'd read a little bit about Bob Marshall and have learned more since. Marshall was one of the founders of the Wilderness Society, the society responsible for pushing the Wilderness Act through Congress in 1964. He was also one of the most passionate voices for preserving land in the 1920s and '30s. Though he grew up in a wealthy New York Jewish family, he spent his adult life in Idaho, Montana, and Alaska researching, writing letters, hiking, and making sure the Selway-Bitterroot and other wild lands were never developed.

"If it wasn't for Bob, there'd be a goddamn road right down the Selway River," Dick said.

He stooped and pulled a slimy, larval, rusty brown cone from the creek. "It's a catkin." And he placed it in my open palm. Was it some kind of insect? I was afraid to ask, ashamed of my ignorance of the natural world, though I felt the magic of whatever it was, cool and wet against my skin.

"Your grandad may have known Bob," he said. "I got a letter somewhere. George wrote it when Bob died, wrote as if he knew him."

I asked what the letter said.

"Well, the Selway-Bitterroot Wilderness was supposed to be named the Bob Marshall Wilderness. Because the Selway, it was Bob's favorite place." Bob wanted to build huts in the wilderness, Dick said. To make it available to people who were too poor to come otherwise. George was trying to fulfill that wish.

As Dick talked, a proud feeling about George bloomed inside me for the first time. I was sensing the currency of being his granddaughter in the world of wilderness lovers. But a sour feeling crept behind the pride as we turned to leave. One letter, which Dick eventually read to me on the phone and which I never actually laid eyes on, wasn't much proof of anything. Besides, George had shut my mother out of the wilderness and made my grandmother miserable, whatever that meant.

Back at the house, we had kale slaw and strong coffee. As I packed my bag to go, Dick disappeared down the hall and came back with a leather-bound book. "Have you seen these?" He held the book open and turned the pages slowly. I gasped. There were my grandparents standing on the airfield of Moose Creek Ranger Station—Esther, tall and thin in a gingham cotton dress with a white broadcloth collar, and George, shorter by a foot, in jodhpurs and black boots looking as if he'd just stepped out of World War I. The two of them filled page after page: he on skis along a snowy mountainside trail; she by a vegetable garden holding a baby or bathing a child in a metal washtub; he standing on a tree stump holding a bear skin—the very photo I'd spotted in Esther's album when I was sixteen. The same album I'd held in my teenage hands seemed to have somehow made it to Dick's house.

"Where'd you get these?" I asked.

Dick brushed back his thick gray hair and sighed.

I had taken the album from Dick and was turning the pages. Not only did Esther not burn the photos, but she actually looked happy, or at least not unhappy—leading a child on a horse in one, smiling with her head relaxed and cocked sideways in another. Maybe her scribble on the photo I'd found in her box about her *many miserable years* was the product of a moment, not a lifetime.

"These are our family heirlooms," I said, glancing back and forth between the album and Dick as if I'd just discovered a crime. I closed the book, looking at Dick harder than I meant to. Dick, the rogue archaeologist, the Indiana Jones of Moose Creek.

I wanted to know how he had come to possess the photos. I felt they were rightfully mine. I even had the urge to return them to my mother, perhaps as a way to atone for the throb of guilt I now felt for assuming she had kept them from me. But I looked around and knew there was a lot more to uncover not only in the house but in Dick himself. I didn't want to jeopardize the connection. I handed the book back to him, and we made plans for me to visit the following week.

Driving home in the dark, I tried to get my head around who Dick was and tried to be angry that he had Esther's photos. But all I saw was an avalanche of glacier lilies spilling over a green hillside, and all I felt was gratitude.

10 Constellation

Summer, 2018. It seems more than a coincidence that a month before Connie went missing, I was on a small commuter boat with a seventy-year-old woman, white hair and round red cheeks, whose name I never did learn. A cobalt yoga mat propped next to her deepened her blue, shining eyes. A wobbly table as you'd see in a diner was wedged between us. She reached across and touched my hand as a mother would. I accepted the gesture of this stranger as the water grew choppy.

I was on my way to a writing workshop at a retreat center on Cortes Island, British Columbia. I had enrolled in the workshop in order to finally organize the wilderness notes, documents, and stories I'd been col-

Beach at Cortes Island, 2018. DJ Lee photo.

lecting over the years into a narrative, though I can't explain why I chose that specific workshop at that particular time. The woman was going to a constellation workshop.

I'd never heard of it.

"Like astrology?" I said.

"Nothing like that," she said. "It's the most marvelous experience." It was hard to explain, she confessed, but then she went on to describe it in vivid detail as if it wasn't hard at all.

"Our ancestors have issues," she said, "and these issues interrupt the family energy field." She leaned, as if in confidence, though the boat carried no one else except the driver. "Just like when a tree is stunted, it grows in a gnarly, wounded kind of way. A family can develop like that over centuries." Her hair was bundled into a fuzzy donut on the top of her head. It wiggled as the boat bobbed and heaved.

There's a protocol to constellation work, she went on. Participants, total strangers to one another, are asked questions by a facilitator, questions like: Who in your family died early, died in childbirth, committed a serious crime, committed suicide? Who was murdered, abandoned, isolated, excluded, abused, wrongly accused, institutionalized? Who simply disappeared? With these ancestors in mind, one person at a time assigns roles to other workshop participants. The role players act out the situation based on what they feel in the moment.

As she was explaining, she seemed to sense my skepticism through my narrowed eyes, but also my fascination. I know the power of watching a live play. I've experienced improvisational theatre. I tried to envision a spontaneous scene between Esther, George, and the Wilderness, to see them standing on stage in an unfolding performance. I had no idea where the scene would go.

"It sounds strange," she said, "but in the re-enactment, a whole new energy field is created. People take on roles of ancestors or family friends, even living relatives, parents, siblings, uncles and aunts, and grandparents. They inhabit these roles though they know nothing about the situation."

I noticed her large, cradle-like arms freckled against her sleeveless purple smock. Earrings of tiny silver fish curling into themselves. "The point is to remember those who have been excluded and bring them back

into the family, into the community, and in so doing, to heal the disturbance," she said. "Like pasts reborn in different lives."

I was still thinking of my family, of the wilderness, the topic I'd come
to the retreat center to write about. "What if a whole history has disappeared?" I asked. "What if a whole landscape is a mystery?"

"It's the same," she said. "The constellation principle applies to histories and places."

She said that I should really think about switching workshops.

When we arrived at the retreat center, I was confronted with a wild
mix of people: young women in tie-dye skirts, older women just finding
themselves, single young men and single older men, couples, children,
African drummers, painters, and poets. It felt liberating, and I had high
expectations. But in my writing workshop and in the solitary effort in my
cabin beside a hemlock forest, I couldn't stay on task of organizing my
notes, many of them based on stories Connie had related and experiences
I'd had with her. I didn't know how to write about a place so complex,
crossed with so many people's lives. I stared at the blank computer screen,
drifting back like waves on an ocean to what the woman on the boat told
me, how we relive our mother's anxieties, repeat our father's disappoint-
ments, replicate the failed relationships of our grandparents.

There are events beyond a person's life that define their story, the
woman had said. Her own grandparents got pregnant before marriage, a
taboo at the time, lost the family farm, and were forced to emigrate from
Ireland to Canada. "Even though my children's children may never know
that story, they can't reach their full potential, their full flowering, with
our ancestors' story floating around unresolved. It's a sort of secondary
PTSD. This can happen," she said, "on a cultural level, too, so that whole
nations need to be healed." A woman she knew had suffered from claus-
trophobia so intense she was unable to ride in a plane or elevator. During
constellation, this woman made the connection to her father's parents
who'd perished in a gas chamber.

In the evenings, there was a luminous full moon, driftwood for miles,
and the Salish Sea filled with bioluminescence, a million stars floating
in the dark water. One night the woman from the boat coaxed me into
swimming naked at midnight in the cold salt tide with other partici-

pants, singing, laughing. At lunch the next day, I happened to sit next to the constellation facilitator, Jill, a voluptuous woman with kind eyes. Her husband, the controversial Cambridge biologist Rupert Sheldrake, mixer of scientific and spiritual traditions, pioneer of morphic resonance—a process whereby each individual inherits a collective memory from past members of its species as well as contributes to the collective memory of the future—sat by her side. Jill's sense of family constellation, I gathered from the conversation and from what I read later, was one version of morphic resonance. She talked about inherited trauma. She said traumas live on long after the original event, and, for whatever reason, some people in subsequent generations resonate with a particular ancestor or trauma and carry it for the family. Most of the time, the original ancestor in question has been excluded and needs to be brought back into the family.

"But what's miraculous," Jill said as she stirred her soup, "is that the person who resonates with the original trauma is the very person chosen to heal it."

Was I that person? I didn't switch workshops or accomplish much toward organizing my notes, but I left feeling as if I'd been given a message about my narrative.

11 Collage

Sometimes I see my mother as the glossy center of a dozen Russian nesting dolls: I open and open and open until I reach the source, the one that doesn't split in half, the solid one. Sometimes she's the seam binding each square of fabric on the quilts my grandmother made from recycled clothes. Or, she's the whole quilt. In each of these pictures, my mother has

Shirley Case, 1958. Family photo.

the hardest stare I've ever encountered, the look that shoots deep and can undo me.

In 1999, when Esther had her stroke, my mother and I took turns visiting her in the St. Maries Care Center. In fact, we were never there at the same time. It was better that way. On one of my visits, I noticed something new on the wall of Esther's room. My mother had created a photo collage, snapshots of my three brothers, their wives, and their children glued on a sheet of twenty-by-twenty-inch cardboard. There was a photo of my bachelor uncle, Richard, the

bearded one with the blurry, crooked face and glass eye, and images of Aunt Barbara, her husband, their children, and their grandchildren. My father was represented. So was Myron, with his big, open smile and his arm around my mother. Her fierce black eyes stared straight at me.

But there were no images of me or Steph, who was eleven at the time.

Driving home that evening, I called Myron. "She did it on purpose," I said, outrage spewing into the air as he defended her. Couldn't I understand that Esther's stroke was stressful for my mother? She had a lot of responsibilities, working as a Weight Watcher lecturer, helping to run the family plumbing business.

"You never know," he said. "You haven't lived at home for a long time, she probably couldn't find a photo." That was like him, giving people the benefit of the doubt.

"She knew what she was doing," I said, with conviction.

"You always get so worked up. You'll feel differently later."

No, I wouldn't. I slammed the phone on the seat.

↶

A memory. I'm nineteen years old. I stumble down the stairs with a small table I've used in my bedroom for years. Long curved legs, elegant and strong. Pink. I painted the table salmon pink when I was in middle school. I'm leaving for college and about to angle the table into my car when my mother comes up from behind.

"You can't take that," she says, out of breath, staring me down. She's been watching me from the house, silent and brooding, arms clamped across her chest, and has just now run into the driveway.

I set the table on the gravel drive. "Why not?" Hands on hips, a tingle of resistance runs up my spine.

"It has sentimental value," she says as she grabs it. I grab back, and the table stiffens between us as if guarding itself from destruction.

I don't know what brought us to that point. Maybe my mother was upset at my imminent departure, the terrible ache inside when you want someone to leave and stay at the same time. Maybe I was scared to leave her and was lashing out one last time. Maybe she was envious at my freedom and trying to fight back that unnatural feeling—being jealous of one's own daughter. Her one regret, she told me, was quitting college when she became pregnant with me. But then, as she would sometimes reason, her generation stayed home with children—it was expected. We were in one of our emotional tug-of-wars, and maybe because this one was literal and laced with finality, I fought back directly rather than swallowing what I saw as injustice. I didn't let go of the table.

We jostled and screamed, and the more I pulled, the more she resisted. I argued, "If sentimental value is a condition of ownership, nothing would ever leave our house!" I was thinking about how reluctantly she parted with clothes, books, broken dishes, old records, anything, really, the opposite of my grandmother, who kept nothing.

My mother told me I was possessive. When I wanted something, she reminded me, I would steamroller anyone to get it. "You're just like your father."

Of course, I was just like her, too. Neither of us let go of our opinions or the table—the more power I gathered in my arms and legs and head, the more steam she seemed to muster, until we were both panting.

"It was Esther's," my mother said, finally.

Immediately, I dropped my end. If it was Esther's, my mother was more entitled to it than I was. If it was Esther's, I could see, for a split second, how much my mother needed the solid table. I told myself I didn't care about the old table anyway. But later I cared, and I looked back on the tussle as her attempt to wrench Esther out of my life.

☙

Now, with the poster on Esther's wall, my mother seemed to be cutting me out of my grandmother's visual memory and the family scrapbook.

I planned my revenge.

When I got home that evening, I retrieved a photograph of Esther and Steph from my desk, shot months earlier, before the stroke, when I'd had the day off from the university and had taken Steph out of middle school. Looking at the photograph brought back the day Steph and I pulled into Esther's driveway. The huge walnut tree hung over her rickety porch, which was stacked with bags of thrift store junk as usual. We found her in the backyard by the apple tree using a hoe to snag the branches and draw them low to pick the fruit.

"This is a surprise," she said, pulling us close. I could smell the dry softness of aging skin. The rest of the day we zigged and zagged from one activity to another. Esther enlisted us in apple picking and then peeling the fruit to prepare for canning. Part way into the peeling, we stopped when one of her boyfriends, who at seventy-five was fifteen years her junior, showed up. Esther brought out a flute someone had donated to the thrift store. Steph snapped it together. She had a knack for playing instruments, and she wafted out a couple of soft, silvery melodies. The music made Esther ecstatic. Her eyes sparkled. Her hands flew to her cheeks in amazement. She said, "My, my!" Esther had always associated the sound of live music with transcendence, and when she praised Steph's improvised tunes, I could tell from Steph's wide smile that she felt a little angelic. The boyfriend left. Esther gave Steph a cookbook, also pinched from the thrift store, and talked her through the steps of making apple pie. At some point, Steph climbed the stairs to the attic.

While she was rummaging through what was left of her great-grandmother's treasures, just as I had done at her age, Esther listened to me chatter. I could have said any number of things, about my job, mothering, marriage, even my mother. Mostly, at that time in my life, I couldn't pin down who I was—I seemed to shift and blur and get lost, and sometimes I felt strangled by a kind of ambient despair, so many different directions inside of me, but with Esther, I felt solid, like that girl who'd spent the summer with her. I had raspberries to pick, an attic to explore. I had purpose. As I talked with her, my life seemed to be a painting onto which she had drawn a door. I opened the door, strode out, and could see myself from the outside, as a young mother and college professor following the right path, even if I didn't know where it was leading.

"You'll be fine," she said, handing me a bag of produce, bounty from her garden, to underscore the point. Before we left, I took a photo, Esther's arm threaded through Steph's, as if the two were one, the apple tree glowing behind.

Now, using the photo as a guide, I laid out a sheet of watercolor paper and painted in a loose pointillist technique until the colors muddied, but I got the faces right, Esther's intense eyes and broad nose, my daughter's full cheeks and pencil-thin brows.

On my next visit to the care center, I hung my painting next to my mother's collage. Mine was larger by several inches in each direction. At first I felt avenged, and then a dark and unpleasant mood swept over me because I understood my ham-handed attempt to disrupt the way the two pieces, in their literal flatness, expressed the depth of four generations. My mother's collage, it seemed, caught that expression better. The meaning of us lived in the borders, the interrelationships of the parts, in their juxtaposition, their accumulation, not in the individual images themselves. Even if Steph and I weren't there in photographs, we were everywhere in the spaces between.

"It looks nice," Esther said, speech slurred. I remember considering how my mother would feel when she saw the painting—if Myron was right, she wouldn't notice it at all, but, then again, she might take it as a challenge or a slap in the face, a grief adding to the grief she had already. I was ashamed, but I tried to push that feeling down. I didn't want to hurt my mother, and yet I did, and I couldn't decide which emotion was stronger. I had the urge to take it down right away, but I didn't.

12 Elk

No one knows how memories wind through the mind, get stuck or transform or are forgotten altogether. From time to time throughout my young adulthood, I recalled the blobs I'd seen on the celluloid in Esther's attic at sixteen, but those images faded over time. When the films were missing from the attic the day I visited her house and took the box, I put them out of my mind. They were old films—someone else's memory, a memory of a memory. And then one December, seven years after Esther's death, a slim package arrived at my home bearing no return address. I pulled out a DVD in a black plastic sleeve titled: "George Case Wilderness." A Post-It Note stuck to the front read: "Enjoy, Mom."

By that time, I'd traveled to the Selway-Bitterroot several times and was beginning to grasp what Connie would tell me much later: "All those people in cities, those squished-up places, aren't as intimate as we are in the remote wilderness. There's no common thread. But people in the wilderness, we're connected because we love this place, we share its history, we care about its well-being. Even if we don't see one another often, even if we never meet. We need something from it, and we'll do whatever it takes to get there. We're connected through that need."

My mother and I were very much connected through that need, although we could not express it then. She had also been to Moose Creek and knew about my interest in the place, but never once had she indicated that she had the films. I couldn't blame her. I hadn't told her about Esther's box. What had prompted her to send the DVDs? At first I wondered if it had been a mistake, but then I talked myself out of that idea, accepting the gift as intentional and genuine. I was surprised by how a lifetime of suspicions about my mother, of resentment about her possessiveness,

George Case with elk stranded in snow. Selway-Bitterroot Wilderness. No date.
Courtesy of Dick Walker Historic Photo Collection.

vanished instantly, aware of how provisional my emotional positions could be and how transient hers must be, too. I took the DVDs as an act of grace, a moment of suspension. I can still catch a trace of the love I felt as I unwrapped them.

On one of the dark days after Christmas, I had a break from the university. No one else was in the house. Thick snow covered the ground outside. I was cozied into the living room on a three-legged stool in pajamas and thick socks, stationed a few feet from the TV watching milky black-and-white images from 1930 jerk across the screen: deer moving silently on a ridge, snakes coiling and ready to strike, a bear sunning itself on a grassy mound, chipmunks eating from a man's hand, men felling trees with double-bladed axes, women leading mules across creeks, children running in a snowy forest. Dark dancing against light without chronology. A collage, a constellation.

But the ghostly images flitted by so fast. So I set the DVD to frame-by-frame mode and only then could I begin to see the wilderness as the filmmaker, the young George, had seen it.

Fuzzy black-and-white forest walls. A dark creature crept up a path. The camera followed the creature. Was it a bear? The scene jumped to snowy hills and a dark log. On the log was a coin or a shell. Then: a cut to a pair of overalls hanging from the high branch of a Douglas fir; a bird flew in and perched next to them. George zoomed in on the bird's triangular head and fishy eyes, which there on the screen, in black and white, seemed especially odd. This was not nature romanticized; this was bushy understory, scraggly trees, lonesome snags, empty branches, and animals scratching for food. Unlike early nature documentaries of the 1950s, where animals were portrayed as objects to be killed or collected, George's clips from the 1920s and '30s seemed to let the animals be themselves.

A moose, in one of the only colored movies in the reel, stood knee-deep in a crystal-blue lake, head in the water. Its body seemed to be floating. And then it lifted its head, huge antlers silhouetted against the sky, and looked directly into the camera. How strange the animal was, how intimate its gaze, except it appeared fluid, too, like the water it stood in, flowing out of itself, looking from some prehistoric past to a future. George filming the animal, the animal looking through George to me.

"I watched those movies more times than I can count," my mother told me when I stopped the films to call her, to thank her. "I was such a sickly child. I missed so much school. I'd stay home and Esther'd put on those movies. They were my friends. I think that's how the Selway-Bitterroot got burned into my soul."

When Esther died, my mother explained, she took the 16 mm films from the attic and, for years, they sat undisturbed in my teenage bedroom in Spokane Valley. The films were in disarray, many just scraps of two or three frames. "And I got this idea to pay someone to splice them together to give to you children for Christmas."

The generosity of the gesture got to me, the opposite of the table we'd wrenched from one another. It was my mother's way to reveal small stories about her childhood in fragments and crumbs. But now it seemed as if she was piecing together her life and starting to let me in. The world she and I inhabited contracted, grew intimate, as it had the day she told me the Lost Horse story.

"Dad stopped filming just after I was born. It's too bad," she said, voice calm. "He loved that movie camera, but Mother got after him for spending money. You know, he did have a job during the Depression, but the Forest Service didn't pay that much. And, bless his heart, he sent fifty dollars every month home to his mother in Kansas until the day she died. Mother resented that. If it weren't the camera, she would have been on him for something else. She used to say, *There was never a more mismatched couple than George and me.*" My mother laughed dryly.

"Why?"

"Oh, I don't know. If she'd have had some other man, she wouldn't have been happy with him either."

"She was always searching," I said.

"I guess so!" she said.

I could hear her light-heartedness, chittering like a bird, until I said, "Those movies," and admitted how I'd longed to see them as a teenager and had looked for them when Esther died. She grew quiet, and in the quiet I heard smoldering feelings, as if her generosity of sending the DVDs and her need to keep them private were burning against one another, and I regretted I'd said anything. I wanted to drag myself back to the chittering moment, but it was too late.

"I sent a set to Mert," she said, referring to her sister Barbara's husband. "He didn't like them." Her voice took on a plaintive tone, and I braced myself for a mood. "You know what he said to me? *Why did George take all those movies of animals?* How was I supposed to know?" she said.

I leapt to her defense before she could unspool the hurt. "I see why he took them. Wild animals were his neighbors. His social world. He was an early wildlife documentary filmmaker."

Silence. Then: "I never thought of it that way," she said brightly, and we hung up, each having given something to the other through George.

⌇

The mismatched couple, George and Esther, were on screen in two or three clips lasting mere seconds. Esther, who looked to be thirty, dark hair and a stiff back, entered the screen and threw a bitter glare, brows sinking into sharp eyes. George filmed himself only once or twice, skiing down a small mound in the wilderness or leading a mule team.

I kept looking for more people, moving images of my mother, Esther, George himself. But it was elk George returned to again and again, elk herds supplanting our familial past. Elk eating mountain mahogany or bedded down in a meadow or chewing dirt at a salt lick. He filmed elk herds swaying, loosening, tightening, accordion-like, as they ran across a snowy savannah. Their energy was collective, communal, like the wilderness itself, a language of strength and instinct.

The films had the feel of memory's moments, past and present, except unlike memories, which can be fleeting, unstable, vapid, the films could be rewound, replayed exactly as they were, examined and analyzed, and they didn't rupture into disturbances and threats. Even so, I've come to think of them as a mode of thought, the way they fade and flashback—a permeable boundary between George's memory and the collective memory of the wilderness.

When I finally turned off the films that December day, I moved from the three-legged stool to the sofa. I needed time. The world was turning on a new axis. I still didn't know much about George, but after seeing the films, I realized I'd thought of him as unrefined, half-literate, half-ghost, half-human. Maybe he was those things, but he was an artist, too.

13 Wilis

October 20, 2018

A tent, stove, ice chest, axe, sleeping bag, portable table, chair, and solar charger are permanently stashed in the back of my car, and on a Saturday, I set off for the wilderness, driving southeast from my house through stubbled wheat fields. Behind my concentrated gaze Connie wanders the forest in a bounce. I hear strands of her voice, its slightly nasal quality, how she pronounces her words intently with a quiet, green edge, how she breaks midsentence, not in an act of forgetting or wanting for words, but to let the brokenness speak for itself.

Before I know it, I'm in Lewiston, dry hills and fertile valley on the Snake and Clearwater Rivers, stench from the pulp mill hanging in the air. I pass other vehicles, drivers staring through windscreens, dead eyed, and turn onto Highway 12, where trees narrow the road on one side and the backbone of the Clearwater squeezes the other.

Years earlier, when I visited Connie at her home in Nezperce on Idaho farmland not far from where I'm driving now, she seemed small. She is actually quite tall—especially compared to me—but I'd only ever seen her in the wide expanse of the wilderness, never in a domestic setting. She sat on a sofa by the fire, cat curled on the rug. When I commented on the moose replicas scattered throughout her house—a moose-shaped pillow on the sofa, moose salt-and-pepper shakers on the table, a moose clock above the door jamb, a moose head on a toilet paper roll cover on the tank, she said, "They call me Momma Moose, because I lived there at Moose Creek all those years." But she was less a Momma Moose than an observer of the real moose, and the replicas seemed cheap and odd in the context of her rich stories.

"Moose are my favorite," she said. "They're an enigma. They show up in the weirdest places and do such unexpected things. One time I was at the station alone and this momma moose came in with a bull moose following close on her heels. It was during estrous for her, and for the next three days, they mated. Constantly. And then one morning I woke up and there was blood all over the ground. I investigated and it was clear that another animal hadn't died there—that was obvious. I knew it was some mark of animal life, some mark of love. Makes you think about the mystery of life that thrives in that place, and there I was, a lowly human, trying to figure out what happened."

I reach Three Rivers, where the Lochsa and Selway Rivers meet to form the Clearwater. I turn up the road, and soon the pavement gives way to gravel. The road follows a series of hills on one side, a steep drop into the Selway on the other. My thoughts drop, swirling in the current.

More news about Connie has arrived this week: She was alone in the hunting camp. She contacted the hunters by radio on October 3, a Wednesday, but they couldn't make out what she was saying, and then the line dropped. I replay the interview with the Idaho County sheriff, his face crushed and long, flipping his head around, a whine in his voice, saying the area where Connie was last seen is covered in blowdowns—trees and brush in a tangle left after severe wind and snowstorms, terrible terrain to travel in.

I bump along for eighteen miles until I reach the rough road up to Fog Mountain Saddle and the long trail to Big Rock. A metal gate bars drivers from the mountain, says the road is closed. I park and tramp around, confused, as if I've forgotten what I'm looking for, pocketing a few pieces of charred pine bark, sidestepping a wild raspberry bush, its thorns bared. A streak of cloud passes overhead, dimming the sun. Shudder.

Attached to the gate is a sign—Missing, October 5, 2018—and a photo of Connie against a background of green, eyes squinted in a smile, and Ace, the black-and-white border collie, lying in a curl, ears folded back, the face of adoration. A number to call if anyone has information. The laminated sign, new and fresh, like "The bridge at Dog Creek is out" sign she had picked up deep in the wilderness, has me rewinding to the instant when Connie called the hunters on the shortwave radio. I realize it's magical thinking, but I imagine this time they can make out her scratchy voice behind the static, can rescue her.

I swing my car around. A quarter mile away I set up camp in a wide spot next to the river and a small, noisy stream, Gedney Creek. The water's low, leaving rocks bared, jagged and hungry, like teeth.

I hear it before I see it, a pickup speeding by, the driver a man with an ashen face and long beard. I recall what a friend of mine and Connie's wrote to me a few days earlier: "Useless to speculate, but I've seen some sketchy people at the Fog Mountain Trailhead."

The man slows down. Waves. A hunter. He keeps driving. Dust lingers. Nothing to fear, I whisper to no one. I've been coming here all autumn with the salmon run, the falling leaves, the river draining away. I haven't been afraid.

Time to make firewood. Heave the blade through a log and it cries out in ropy chunks. I strike again and again until I have a sufficient pile. Sweating, I discard my coat and mosey down to the river. Carved by water and shaped by rock, the bed is a tangle of forms. The sun reflects off small puddles, illuminating plants, insects—no-see-ums, flies, bees—and sand flecked with lode and placer gold, a few freckles of plastic left by hunters or hikers, and scales from steelhead, Chinook, rainbow and cutthroat trout. A Forest Service hydrologist once told me that the Selway is the most pristine river in the country outside of Alaska, meaning the least contaminated as measured in parts per million. As it trickles and skips, I listen for it to tell me something. But it's mercurial. It doesn't give up its secrets easily.

A big tree, a Douglas fir, could simply bury a person. A 150-foot green cedar weakened by fire fell and struck a young woman firefighter several years back. A memorial tree is planted in a park not far from my house. But no. Ace would sense the coming destruction the way animals know what humans do not, would have felt the earth tremble and the roots letting go. Ace would have warned her.

"The same day Connie disappeared," my mother had said, "another man vanished not twenty miles away. He was on a film crew making a movie. No one knows what happened to him, but there are some old mine shafts in that area, and I wonder if he fell into one. And then another woman, I can't remember her name, went missing. That one was foul play.

I suspect her husband. Connie, though, I don't think she had an enemy in the world. You hate to see anyone come to a tragic end, and it's worse when they're a beautiful person."

I head up the road a half mile, then wander back down when an owl *whoo-hoos* me home. I build a fire, snuggle up to it. A breeze stirs, something rustles, and I think of the whoosh of wilis, the ghosts of maidens who haunt the roadways and black nights of European folklore. In some of these shifting mythologies, wilis are nymphs, protectors of the forest, have power over wind and storms. Or they are fairy creatures wearing skirts of leaves, veils of water, gowns of smoke, living in clouds, rivers, or caves. They're shapeshifters, mistresses of transformation, can appear as birds or wolves or humans. Their voices resemble mountain woodpeckers. They can be restorative, healing wounded animals like deer and foxes, can tell the future, and sometimes they will help humans. Wherever they dance, they leave behind a ring of grass. Because they dwell between this world and the next, they can be capricious, vengeful, and mean just as easily as healing and kind.

They love dogs above all other animals.

When my father first called me and after I hung up, I had the romantic idea that Connie had gone into the woods to die, to merge with the place she called home. But when cool globes of mist land and break on my glasses, I feel she did not end it herself. She wanted to live, may still be alive.

At 6:00 p.m. it's dark except for a blue edge on the mountaintops and cold stars stabbing the sky. If not for the fire, the dew coating the grass, rocks, trees, and me would be unbearable. Smoke rises in thick rivulets then vanishes. I shift in my chair as dampness penetrates my bones. *Honestly, we don't know.* I fight against the not-knowing. Gedney Creek rattles on.

14 Cycle

A Chinook salmon is designed for transformation. It changes body states five times throughout its life. The coveted fish starts as a redd, a fertilized egg planted in the rocks of a river in late spring or early fall by a spawning female. Over the winter, as the egg gestates and hatches, it becomes an avelin, a tiny being with a bubble-like stomach. When it emerges from its gravel bed, it turns into a fry, a mere sliver of a thing. The fry lives from one to three years in the river, darting in and out of boulders, camouflaging with sun and shadows, feeding on plants and insects as it grows from two centimeters to four or five. And then one day it gets an ancient urge

"The Origin Point," Nimíipuu tipi, 1926. Van Emerson photo.
Courtesy of Nez Perce-Clearwater National Forest.

to migrate to the ocean. It floats—it's now called a smolt—down creek and stream and river to the sea, where it stays for three to five years in its saltwater home, growing, maturing, and putting on fat and muscle as it becomes a salmon.

A salmon is a homing organism, its whole life pointed to the future through the past. While the smolt journeys to the ocean, she enacts a process called retracing imprinted memory. Every body of water, every river, creek, stream, and trickle, has its own taste, and the smolt memorizes the tastes written into the chemistry of each water system. This knowledge enables her to find her way back home.

Dick Walker was obsessed with the Selway Chinook. He explained the creature's life cycle over and over until I knew it by heart, until the births, transformations, and migrations felt like my own. The magical part, the part of their lives I kept mulling over, was the Chinooks' treacherous voyage from the ocean back to the exact spot where they were born. Salmon swimming up, river flowing down, a perfect tension.

I ended up spending countless hours with Dick after that first meeting, learned the meandering route to his house, where to turn, speed up, slow down, always with a carton of kale slaw and a bottle of gin. On weekends when Myron was working out of town (Steph was in college in Canada), I often drove to "Pecker Flats," as Dick called his cabin because it was four miles from the town of Peck. Dick may have acquired Esther and George's photographs, by what means I never did learn, but as we spent time together, he opened his archives to me.

Every month or so, Dick flew his 170 Cessna on missions for wilderness advocacy groups, the Nimíipuu, or the Forest Service to study wild animal habitat, take aerial photographs, or spot fires. Sometimes he flew in just to land at Moose Creek airfield to photograph and listen to wolves howl, and sometimes he let me come along. Though I knew Dick wasn't my grandfather, I often felt that by following him around, I was walking in George's shadow. So much so, that no matter what I was doing, if Dick called, I would pick up. If he asked me to come on a flight, I'd do everything in my power to be there.

One August, I was sitting in front of a slot machine at the Las Vegas airport when Dick's name flashed across the phone. "I just talked to the fisheries biologist," he said, voice taut and hard. "There's hundreds of salmon swimming up the Selway right now. Can you be here tonight?" I was on my way to Salt Lake for a literature conference, but Dick's urgency became my own. "This is going to be the year!" he said.

"I'll be there." I hung up and stared at the slot machine with a cartoon rendition of Princess Leia from *Star Wars* holding a big ray gun, pulled around by fear and doubt at my willingness to change my plans so readily. But I had wanted to see the salmon ever since I'd helped Dick hang a photography exhibit at a café near the university the previous year. His portraits of animals in the wild captivated me: a brown bear cruising up a path in Alaska, wolverine tracks in the snow somewhere in the Bitter-roots, a moose and her calf barely visible through the fog at Fish Lake. Dick didn't turn the animals into sumptuous images to be consumed. He wanted to show their vulnerability. For this reason I was skewered by the image of a half-dead, half-living salmon swimming in an emerald pool, the flesh on its head eaten away.

"That time's gone," Dick said as we hung the print. "That's a spring Chinook. If you really look, you see that fish has its adipose fin. That means it's fucking wild. It wasn't clipped in some goddamned hatchery. And this one isn't even a true wild Chinook, since the salmon that come now were taken from another water system after the original Chinook died in the fucking dams."

"What happened to its head?" I asked.

"Probably got nitrogen poisoning or caught in a gill net. I don't know if it was he or she, but I call it she. She came so close to me because she was blind. All the flesh on her face, even her eyes, gone. Her head was nothing but bone and cartilage. That fish came through all those mean-ass rapids, maybe nine hundred miles, and didn't have no fucking eyes. You know what that means?"

I shook my head.

"You don't have to see to get back to the place you were born." He breathed heavily, and then his face brightened into a smile.

"Where'd you take this?" I asked.

"On a bluff overlooking a pool. Lookee here." He pointed to the bottom right-hand corner, where he'd signed his name and penciled in *Upper Selway*.

"This pool here," and he swirled his hand near the print, "I call it the

Origin Point. It's a Nez Perce fishing spot." His voice grew stern. "I don't want people knowing where this place is, so I just write *Upper Selway*. Leave it vague. I wanna keep it that way."

"Dick," I said, "very few people are going to take the trouble to visit a place like that. Think about it." I told him it took longer and was more trouble to get from New York City to the Upper Selway than from New York City to Bamako or Sydney or Cairo or just about anywhere. "You're paranoid."

"No." He strutted away. "I'm not paranoid. I'm a fucking realist." Then he pivoted toward me and his scowling face said, "You have a lot to learn." With anyone else, I would have been hurt by such abruptness. But Dick and I had developed a friendly combativeness, roughing one another up intellectually, while underneath we had respect, care, for one another. In our own clumsy ways, we were inching one another toward a deeper connection to the Bitterroots.

A few weeks after we hung the print, Dick flew me into the wilderness to see the spawning Chinook. They were already gone. This time, Dick promised, would be different. The salmon would be there, he was sure of it.

I arrived at his house at midnight, exhausted, and still dismayed at how quickly I'd reversed my flight and cancelled my plans for the chance to see the vanishing Chinook. Dick was already asleep downstairs. I let myself in. A tin cup of whiskey waited for me on the bedside stool, as usual. The next day, Dick and I were in Orofino, ten miles from his cabin, wheeling his Cessna out of the hangar. Silver with red letters, the plane seemed to have come straight out of World War II, not a fighter jet but a small spotter plane, where you might see daylight through the door. We packed carefully to balance the weight.

"Eight-Zero-One-Nine Alpha. Departing runway two-seven, heading over the reservoir," Dick whispered into the microphone poised on his lips. He slipped a hand from the steering gear to a red knob feebly attached to the dashboard, and we lifted off. Takeoffs always meant flying low into Dworshak, the massive seven-hundred-foot concrete gravity dam on the Clearwater River, the largest of its kind in the Western hemisphere, built during the Cold War as a demonstration of the brute power of American technology.

Flying straight at Dworshak was terrifying every time.

Dick hated the dam, blamed it for salmon loss. As he'd explained, when a smolt makes its way to the ocean, it doesn't swim, it floats. It needs an unhurried but steady pace, the pace of a free-flowing river, to transform its body chemistry from a freshwater into a saltwater creature. The process requires a delicate balance between osmotic pressure and urinating body salts. Dams slow rivers, disrupt this process, and salmon die. Fewer smolt in the ocean mean fewer salmon returning to the Selway.

We rose above the dam and it disappeared. Relief was palpable in the small cabin. Forest fire smoke clouded the sky as we passed over the pinprick town of Weippe, where the Nimíipuu had rescued Lewis and Clark from starvation in 1805, and then over the Lochsa, where Colgate, the cook abandoned by hunters in 1893, had once camped in a snow hole. Patches of clear-cut and farms morphed into mountains, trees, and granite rocks. Dick's green baseball cap shaded his forehead as he eyed the camera dangling from my neck.

"Open the window," he said. I hesitated, but his look said, "Open it!" so I did. The wind whooshed in. "Shoot," he said. With Dick watching me, I felt blundering—and frightened—as I stuck the front part of my face outside the window, held the viewfinder to my eye, and snapped. When I pulled the camera back in, I realized I'd been holding my breath, literally and figuratively. I was expecting something to happen, some big revelation, ever since I'd left Vegas.

The mountain skyline came into view, silhouetted against the smoky horizon. Dick tilted the plane to a forty-five-degree angle, and the skyline melted into the quicksilver of the Selway River. He pointed out his personal landmarks: "That's Wylie's Peak. The lookout was built in nineteen twenty-seven but it burned in nineteen eighty-three. There's Grotto Lake. I came in there in sixty-nine. It's not even on the topo. And there's Boyd Lake. That's not on the map either. That's Big Rock where there used to be a lookout . . ." It was the first and only time I saw Big Rock, the place where Connie would disappear years later, and I remember only a bald mountain with a giant fin of granite poking through the center.

The valley narrowed and a small creek splintered from the Selway. "Here we are," Dick said, turning sharply so I could photograph the secret place from above. But as I stuck my camera out the window once again, the plane bucked, tossing my shoulder against the flimsy door. It felt as if we were falling out of the sky. "The air's getting squirrelly." Dick said, angling the plane toward the river.

A harsh grind came from beneath my feet. Metal on metal. "What was that sound?" I shouted, panic in my throat.

"The engine!"

"Are we going to be able to land?"

"I don't fucking know!" he snapped, knuckles white on the steering mechanism.

"I'm totally cool with whatever," I summoned the courage to say, a bet against crashing. The plane jerked us side to side for seconds that lasted hours. My mind went blank, my body numb, as the world spun into chaos.

And then, somehow, Dick lifted out of the canyon. I have no idea what maneuver he made or which buttons he pressed. All I remember is that the air grew still, and a few minutes later, we were touching down on the Shearer airstrip, a Forest Service outpost fifteen miles upriver from Moose Creek. Shaken and completely astonished to be alive, I was high on the pleasure of a close call coursing through my veins. We were tying down the plane when another aircraft approached and landed, and out popped Joe. The world of backcountry western pilots is small. Dick and Joe shook hands, exchanged stories. Dick told Joe we were on the hunt for spawning Chinook.

"I was up there a few weeks ago," Joe said, in a sauntering voice, his huge mustache moving with his story. "I was flyin' over the hole and saw some pretty big bodies in there. I made a quick U-turn and landed on the airfield, threw an underwater camera and a fly pole in my daypack, and started up the trail. When I got to the bluff, I could see maybe twenty-five to thirty-five salmon. I was so excited, I ripped off my clothes, grabbed my camera, and plunged in, but," he paused and cracked a sly smile, "they weren't all that receptive to having their picture taken. They hadn't spawned and they were strong. I mean, I even saw 'em coming out of the water fighting. They had some pretty big teeth." Joe was referring to the sharp teeth male salmon develop to kill competitors during mating.

The image of big teeth and big bodies jolted Dick into action. "We gotta boogie!" he said. We had five miles of backpacking ahead of us.

The trail to the Origin Point ends at a moss-covered granite bluff seventy-five feet above the water. When we were within a half mile, unable to contain myself, I ran ahead of Dick, dropped my pack, and peered over the edge. The water was sapphire and smoke, rippling where it touched the bluff. I squinted and stared. "We missed them again!" I called out, and felt myself adjusting to a new version of the Origin Point and of myself. Was I right to want the creatures so desperately? Getting close to wildlife through Dick held the promise of getting close to George and his love of wild creatures.

A few minutes later, Dick stepped onto the bluff and squatted beside me. "There they are," he said in a quiet, musical, voice.

"Where?"

"Right below us."

I gazed again into the water, beholding only a surface mottled with sun and shadows. Dick kept looking. I followed suit. Nothing. Then, a dark body came into view. A few more appeared. They hovered in one place. They darted through the water. They disappeared. One of them shot to the surface, a metal glint from his open mouth, and lunged back down. "They're huge!" I said.

Dick pulled out his camera and clicked away. The world felt small and quiet.

"What're they doing down there?" I said. "What kinds of fishy thoughts are going through their brains? Is coming home to the place you were born a party, or is it sad, like the last breath before death?"

"Oh no, there's no sadness." He was perched on the edge, leaning over a little too far, one hand balancing on the mossy rock, the other holding his camera.

"It probably feels good," I said. "A family reunion."

"I don't know." He looked skyward, squinting. "Could be."

Dick began singing softly, "Swing low, sweet chariot . . ." and, as he held the camera to his eye, he mumbled something about being carried home. *Click, click.* "Yeah, I'm getting some good shots. You can see the spots on their backs."

"They look content," I said.

"This would be, in our terminology, a spa life."

"Spawn life?" I punned.

"Well," he snapped the lens cap onto his camera, "the gravel is their last big hurrah. She and the male are separated, and she starts shaking, it's like a mini orgasm, and then he wiggles and shivers, and they're not touching, but they feel each other's vibrations."

He stopped talking, we both did. He put his camera away, and we sat there in a feeling too big for words.

Half an hour later, down at the beach, I dropped my pack and leaned against it, exhausted from our record pace and our salmon-watching, but Dick kept his pack on, poking around in the sand with a stick, shuffling like a dog preparing to bed down. He motioned me over and pointed to a brick wall, ankle-height, built into the side of the earth. "This may be a Nez Perce fireplace."

I studied it. A couple of bricks, fire-scarred, rounded and worn, half covered in sand, trying to train my eye to the cracked markers, astonished at how these rocks buried in plain sight now radiated significance. "Do you think George ever came here?" I said.

"Beats me," Dick said. He knew I wanted to make meaning, and he resisted. There was a lesson there. He was teaching me to hold my narratives, not impose them on the wild. He stretched his arms overhead and smiled widely. "Now get out your Thermarest."

I frowned.

"No," he said with a soft grin. "We ain't gonna nap. We're gonna float."

Minutes later, our inflated mattresses were casting shades on the water, cutting the glare and creating a window into life under the surface. Dick took one float and then went ashore. I couldn't get enough. I lay on my belly, face peeping over the mattress edge, as still as possible while I glided right over the top of the salmon, who were almost as long as I was. Slimy, murky, rhino-colored creatures, they wiggled their tails against a soft current but paid me no mind. They were close and yet remote, so many life forms away. How distant the rest of the world felt as I watched my own shadow over the salmon moving like ribbons in the wind.

While I floated, Dick, barefoot, ambled up and down the shore photographing and gathering three log poles from debris that had washed down the creek. He bound them together with rope to create a tee-pee where we would sleep.

Later, he built a small fire on the beach propped between two slabs of granite and we ate dinner. "I hate big-ass fires," he said. The coals turned organ-red and spit blue flame as we talked into the night. "There was one small band of Nez Perce a long time ago," he said. "The Ne'hu-lat-poe. This whole area was their origin point. It must have been one unbelievable gathering spot. The salmon you see up in Alaska and British Columbia now, we had it here at one time, see, but we don't have that nutrient pool anymore—it's gone."

Gone. I wanted to share his sadness, except all I could feel was the joy of the salmon rising and sinking and swirling in ardent, shifting patterns.

In the morning, the water was mirror-slick. Dick, wearing a lime-green parka and a blue stocking cap from his river-running days, poured coffee and we packed up. "It seemed like I was up all night listening to this little creek," he said. "It does lots of talking. There's murmurs, and then there's burps, and then there's the constant gray fall. And I think in the background, a couple of times, I heard a great horned owl."

"I dreamt of food," I said, wrapping my hands around a large mug. "Lemon tarts, brownies, cherry pie, and zucchini stuffed with cream cheese, and a huge banquet table with silver and crystal and silk."

When Dick didn't answer, I grew uncomfortable. "I guess that's a metaphor for hunger," I said, forcing a laugh.

"No," he said. "You just miss civilization." I read annoyance, scorn, in his squint. "You'll get to a supermarket soon enough."

Dick and I had mastered the art of throwing challenges at one another, but this time I felt gut-punched, could hardly speak. A burning shame flooded in. How would I ever feel at home in the wilderness—my natal waters—if my subconscious longed for fancy dinners, he seemed to be saying. "I'm a homing organism, too," I said. "I'm trying to understand this place. I'm trying hard."

Dick nodded and sauntered off. I wanted to protest, but I saw myself running up to him and fumbling for words, platitudes and excuses falling to the ground and Dick trampling right over them. I swallowed the thought and let it give way to a strange feeling, yearning flecked with suspense and grief.

Spawn life.

Dick and I flew to the front country in silence. Though I stared out the window, taking in the mountains and miles and miles of trees disappearing into a horizon of blue, I was replaying the scene on the bluff overlooking the salmon, Dick and I perched on the edge. "The female releases a hundred eggs," Dick had said, waving his arm like a fishtail. "She burrows into the gravel violently to cover the eggs and immediately squirts out another batch. The male fertilizes the eggs and she blasts the gravel up again." They perform this dance twenty or thirty times until her eggs are gone, he said, and then, exhausted, both male and female repair to the edge of the creek to die. Their corpses, rich in nutrients, nourish the surrounding water, animal, and plant life long into the future. A tree might feed off one salmon carcass for hundreds of years. Along some riverbanks, scientists had found salmon DNA at the top of some of the tallest trees.

"There's so much primal stuff that's totally beyond us in the wilderness." That was Dick's mantra, one I heard countless times. Wilderness protection wasn't perfect, but it preserved animal and plant habitat and the mysteries of the living Earth, like homing movements of salmon and people. Dick was convinced that we wouldn't survive as a species unless we learned Earth was a sentient being. The more I was around Dick, the more convinced I was, too.

15 Parachute

Just as my mother had watched George's films repeatedly as a child, I replayed them on my laptop for years until they rolled across the screen of my mind, in the foreground or in the background on continuous loop. The films were so squarely in this world that they seemed out of this world, the way my grandfather framed small processes like sharpening an axe or gave the simplest of gestures like bathing a child a kind of awe, the way the images stuttered and jerked, offering fleeting glimpses with perfect grace. I felt the raw effects of the movie camera perched on a plodding

Ripcord jump with Eagle parachute, Moose Creek Ranger Station, 1940.
Courtesy of Dick Walker Historic Photo Collection.

mule or strapped to my grandfather's body as he skied down a trail, camera imprinting on actual celluloid as the images imprinted on the retinas of my eyes.

↩

A few years after my grandmother's death settled on my mother and me, we were able to talk more frankly about her mental illness. My mother referred to it in bits and pieces—never a long conversation—a snippet here, a reference there, sometimes an anecdote, as if she herself were exploring the events for the first time. She told the stories matter-of-factly, as if mental illness happened to every family. "Oh well," she'd say, unconvincingly, "it's not the worst thing," although she'd felt the stigma of having a mother shattered by insanity, and sometimes I thought that it must have been the worst thing. I asked questions, careful not to pry too deeply and risk my mother's shutting down.

She was fourteen when Esther went to bed and wouldn't get up, tucked into the big bedroom downstairs with three doors. One led to the kitchen, one to the living room, one to the attic. I imagined Esther poised like a spider at the center of the family web. Or was the bedroom Esther's Lost Horse? Today, I reinterpret the scene at Lost Horse that my mother related to me in the Safeway parking lot, thinking Esther may have gone into the woods with a pistol or a knife, planning to end it. Or maybe she was lying exposed, open to the elements, ready for hypothermia to set in. If she'd been delirious, had a psychotic break, or something had taken her to the edge, maybe the mountain air reminded her she had a daughter, my mother, huddled under the car, and came back.

Whenever I thought about my grandmother in the forest, I saw the bears, deer, chipmunks, moose, elk—the subjects of George's films with which I identified when I first watched them—gathered around her in a kind of pastoral fantasy. But the more I studied his films, the more I noticed his fascination with creatures that could take flight: a pileated woodpecker perched in a tree, an owl flying from snowbank to snowbank in an icy river, a flock of ducks lifting off from Daly Lake, and more curiously, airplanes—DC-3s, Travel Airs, Ford Trimotors—soaring through the sky and landing on Moose Creek airstrip, and parachutes, small and large and in between, giving shape to the air.

As Esther was making her first dips toward depression, George, I realized, had an obsession with flight, with floating through atmospheres. His clips of parachutes were mesmerizing, the film blinkering, stuttering like raw nerves, so different from the films of today, skydivers wearing Go-Pros, catching every facial expression, every wrinkle in the jumpsuit, with smooth precision. George shot from above or from below, umbrellas of white against the bright blue, falling in the magic of early film and early flight.

Sometimes, while watching the parachutes in George's silent movies, the beauty and danger inherent in those lacy mushrooms floating toward Earth, I found myself slipping into the shadow of Esther's illness, thinking how her illness was a different kind of fall, not from sky to Earth but an internal descent. My mother said the depression, if that's what it was, may have been caused by her hysterectomy, or it was dormant in her psyche all along, inherited from her father, Edward, the failed farmer, gold miner, and writer. Or it was circumstantial, activated only after she left the wilderness and returned to small town life in St. Maries. In other words, no one knew the cause.

"Grandma went to bed and didn't get up." When my mother first told me this, I thought she meant Esther slept in once in a while, and then I understood it to be literal. My mother's two older siblings, Richard and Barbara, were out of the house by the time Esther crawled into bed. That left my mother to wake up every day to the weight of her mother's illness. When she described Esther as catatonic, I envisioned my mother approaching the bedroom, asking for information adolescent girls need to know: What do you do when you get your period? How do you fit a bra? Or standing in the doorjamb wanting to ask but not knowing how. Esther, unresponsive, lay entangled in the web. The image made me long to travel through time to that bedroom and rescue my mother.

⟜

From what I read in various smokejumping accounts, George was the ranger during the building of a parachute loft and the first fire jump at Moose Creek in 1940, a sort of historic moment in smokejumping history. An army major who had taken a great interest in the smokejumper training witnessed some of the Moose Creek jumping activities, and the practice was soon incorporated into the army's airborne missions in World War II. Even Earl Cooley, one of the Moose Creek smokejumpers, a man highly critical of what he characterized as George's laissez-faire management style, acknowledged my grandfather's place in the history of smokejumping and hinted at his love of the art of parachuting. I've wondered if that love stemmed from the fact that parachutes spoke the language of risk. In George's films, men became tangled in trees, or they missed their marks on the ground, stumbled, and fell. Maybe they broke or sprained bones, it was hard to tell. But if the chute worked, the men glimpsed transcendence with a ripcord and a giant wing guiding them home.

Esther didn't have a ripcord. I can speak about her experience with some authority because when I was in my thirties, a few years after Steph was born, I suffered from a similar depression. Riddled with self-doubt, crying at perceived slights, feeling anxiety and grief over nothing at all, clinging to a person or situation and then pushing that person away, rejecting so as not to be rejected. I was teaching full time, and some days I felt too leaden to get out of bed. I would not have been able to rise at all without Myron pulling back the bedcovers, holding me, standing beside me as I made a sandwich, walking me around the block, helping Steph dress for school. Depression was a battle I fought with Myron's help for most of my adult life.

On more than one occasion, when my mother and I talked about Esther, I would describe what despair felt like, the aura of a migraine without the headache, the cardboard world, the sense of purity during dark insights, the desire to disappear forever. She would nod knowingly and say, "I think I was depressed my whole adult life. That must have been why I cried."

I'll never forget the day that Esther truly descended into Earth, the day of her burial in the St. Maries cemetery. Melting snow muddied the ground around the tombstones. The sky was a sharp blue broken by swirls of cirrus clouds. Twenty-five people gathered around the plot where Esther's ashes were already interred on the same site as George's body was buried. The small children chased one another, climbed on stones and jumped down, screaming with joy. Myron stood close, arm around me.

My father, in a black shirt and sunglasses, thick white hair and trim mustache, was a few plots away at the tomb of one of Esther's many boyfriends. When that boyfriend died ten years earlier, my mother—because he had no living relatives—bought him a tombstone with the inscription: "Loved by Esther." My father now pointed to the stone. "Half the tombstones in this place should say 'Loved by Esther.'" He had enjoyed the richness of her post-George romantic life.

We all laughed.

Then my Uncle Richard, in tweed coat and grizzled beard, his glass eye cocked in a different direction from his reading eye, read a poem by Ralph Waldo Emerson that Esther had expressly asked for.

Loved by Esther.

My mother and I, both selfishly claiming Esther's love for ourselves, were barely speaking that day. When we met at Esther's house after the service, my mother was in the living room giving away the garden hoe to the neighbor. "Thanks for looking in on Mom all these years," she was saying, "you meant so much to her."

Next she turned to one of my cousins. "Mom wanted you to have the organ. Would you like it?"

To another cousin, she said, "This lapis ring was the one good piece of jewelry Mom owned. Do you want it?"

"Wonderful," I said, sarcastically. While my cousins got an organ and a lapis ring, I inherited a family legacy where mothers withheld what their daughters most wanted, and daughters were unable to comprehend their mothers' complex love.

She handed me an umbrella. "Do you remember this?" The umbrella was a green and blue tartan plaid, smaller than the average size, and it leaked, which I knew because it had been mine in middle school. A couple of times every year, we sent Esther bags of old clothing and junk for her thrift store. I must have sent the umbrella; she apparently had rescued it and kept using it for twenty-odd years. "I want you to have this," my mother said.

"That's what you're giving me to remember Grandma?" I said, familiar feelings of resentment and exclusion corkscrewing through me. "My own used umbrella?" She turned away, acting as if she didn't hear me, and maybe she didn't. I ran out of the room fuming, so wounded by the gesture that I couldn't be in my grandmother's house a minute longer. Outside in my thin sweater, my core shivered, my teeth chattered, my fingers froze, but I foolishly refused to go back inside until Myron found me half an hour later and coaxed me up the stairs.

Today, of course, twenty years on and with the benefit of hindsight, it could not be more clear to me why my mother's gift was exactly right. Although she must have been torn in half by sorrow, she had intuited what I couldn't. The umbrella was my inheritance more than anything else Esther owned because a tattered, leaky, secondhand object, useful despite its handicap, was the essence of who my grandmother was, of who we were.

⌒

During one of my discussions with my mother years later, after our relationship started to crack open, I told her I might write about my grandparents, about her, about the wilderness, about Esther's illness. I wouldn't write a linear story. Neither our experiences, nor the wilderness, nor history, nor memory could be held to a narrative straight line.

"It would be more of a collage," I said. "Would you be okay with that?" I braced myself to be cut off or for a flood of tears.

"I don't care," she said, no hint of sarcasm, no binding feeling or holding back. "You can write whatever you want. It's your story." And when she said this, it made me want to protect her, to do the holding back myself, not to give flight to the family constellation, even as I knew I was doing it already and knew I couldn't stop.

Loved by Esther. I saw my mother and me suspended above Earth on two sides of time, and Esther hovering over us like a parachute, or a giant used umbrella.

16 Wilderness Pioneer

The first time I heard Connie's voice was in writing, an email, six years almost to the day after my grandmother died: "You have quite a legacy here in Moose Creek country and I can't wait to hear of the past right out of the mouth of someone closest to the wilderness pioneer George Case," she wrote.

After Joe had mentioned Connie on the ride to Lost Horse and I returned to civilization, I sought her out. A woman in a ranger station somewhere in Idaho gave me Connie's email. I wrote her with some trep-

Esther Case and her daughter Barbara with a Ford Trimotor on Moose Creek airfield. No date. Courtesy of Dick Walker Historic Photo Collection.

idation, asking if I could volunteer at Moose Creek Ranger Station, dropping my grandparents' names as a kind of calling card. In her reply, which came six months later, Connie said I could spend the month of August at the station and, though my exact duties were unclear, I would receive a per diem stipend. I needed to bring my own food and supplies and find my own way into and out of the wilderness—challenges that didn't frighten or surprise me.

What did scare me a little, though, was staying in the very cabin where Esther and George had lived the first twelve years of their marriage, the ranger's dwelling, sleeping in their bedroom. I wasn't easily spooked, but I also wasn't sure I wanted an ancestral visitation. No matter how much I reminded myself that the paths from Esther's box to Dick, to Connie, to the wilderness were fueled by my love for my grandmother and my drive as a scholar to follow leads to their conclusion, I was increasingly bothered by a sense of something bigger in control—synchronicity, or fate, or God. I was hopeful, yet the whole business felt, too, like a venture into a void, into a labyrinth of connections whose endpoint I might never see.

When the time came, my anxiety was whirring at a high pitch. *I can't wait to hear of the past right out of the mouth of someone closest to the wilderness pioneer George Case.* I would have to explain to Connie that I didn't know much about the wilderness pioneer. I could tell her about Esther's box, bring a copy of the *Memoirs*, but she might not care about my memorabilia. I would have to confess that I couldn't tell her much at all, and, actually, *I* was the one who wanted to hear about my family from *her*.

⌁

I reported for duty at Moose Creek Ranger Station in early August as Connie had instructed, having formed an elaborate image of this wilderness celebrity. I imagined her with long dark hair, full lips and ample hips, petite and quick as a squirrel. I was completely wrong, of course.

Joe had flown me in, helped carry my boxes of food, backpack, and a few books from the plane to the porch of the ranger's dwelling. He took off again swiftly, leaving me unsettled since the dwelling was locked and no one was there to greet me. Standing alone in the middle of the wilderness was unlike anything I'd ever experienced to that point—not starting a new high school at seventeen when my family moved from Seattle to Spokane Valley, not living in Arizona with Steph for graduate school while Myron stayed in Washington State, not traveling through Europe alone for my PhD dissertation. This feeling of displacement was sharper, more visceral than those earlier experiences.

I headed up to the main station. That door wasn't locked. Inside, sun glinted through leaded windows, brightening pale yellow walls covered in charts, maps, and informative posters about fish species and noxious weeds. The station had a museum-like quality. A wooden desk, file cabinet, and old-fashioned Singer treadle sewing machine stood about. It was more spacious than I had imagined. From the front office where I stood, I could see a cavernous back room through a patchwork of light and shadows. I managed to croak out a couple of echoing *hellos* and heard footsteps above my head. A few seconds later some large feet in hiking boots landed on the narrow stairs on the other side of the office. I felt even more unqualified than I had earlier, if that was possible.

"In the attic," said a gruff voice, as the speaker came down the stairs—a gangly older man with bald head and thick glasses magnifying round, startled eyes.

Yet he must have been expecting me, because he began talking as if I were a regular visitor as he took off a gauze mask and gloves. I tried not to look surprised myself, stepped forward to shake his hand, but he pulled back. "I'll contaminate you."

Contaminate? He gave me no time to inquire. He led me through the building to the large kitchen with its massive propane-fueled stove, counters big enough to hold a side of elk, and a stainless two-tub sink, where he washed his hands. Danny, as he introduced himself, shared the wilderness ranger job with Connie, and he would instruct me on how to run the station. As we twisted around the place, I was a puppy at his heels, he pointing out shelves of books I could use, food I could avail myself of, propane tanks to hook up when the current one went empty, a root cellar where mule packers kept beer, and so on, until we arrived at another office in which every available surface was covered in cardboard file boxes, piles of loose papers, and books, as if every scrap floating into Moose Creek since 1921, the year it was built, had landed there. I was amused at how the office mirrored the mountains and valleys outside, how it seemed as inscrutable as the land itself, a message in a bottle or Esther's box writ large, and felt immediately drawn to the papers, thinking of the years I'd spent in Cambridge and Oxford and the British Library, reminding me that I was more comfortable in archival mountains and textual forests than in those outside the window.

As if sensing my interest, Danny said, almost proudly, that though it looked chaotic, there was an order to the mess. He closed the door with a sturdy slam and we shuttled around the corner. "This room is Connie's." He tapped a closed, five-paneled door with an iron knob and looked me in the eye for the first time since he'd emerged from the attic. "We don't go in there."

I held back a smile, recalling the reverence with which Joe had intoned Connie's name. Mountain men in deference. I liked Connie more and more. "Where is Connie?" I asked. *Connie*—the word—had such resonance.

"Ah." Danny put his hands on his hips and looked at the ceiling blankly. "She might come."

Might? Connie had said she wanted to hear stories out of my own mouth. Though the idea of teaching her anything still frightened me, I had taken those words to mean she would be here, at Moose Creek. I believed our meeting was destiny. My mind dipped and swerved, assessing what I'd do if she didn't show up. I could assume I would never meet her and let disappointment shake itself out over the next days, or try to forget about her, or—or, possibly, I could learn about her indirectly, the same way as I was learning about my grandfather.

I asked Danny: "What's Connie like?"

He smiled. "Everyone loves her." His tenor implied that he did, too. She was incredibly kindhearted and a damned hard worker, he said, and what appeared to be feminine softness was actually fierceness. "You know," he pushed up the glasses on his nose, "Harrison Ford flew in here last year with a whole entourage of cooks and tents and ass-wipers and whoever he travels with, and Connie marched down the airfield and told him to stop bagging airstrips." He chuckled softly. Bagging airstrips, he explained when I looked puzzled, was a sport practiced by rich pilots, who gathered in remote wildernesses to see how many landings they could make in a weekend. I got an image of Hemingway running with the bulls. It was obnoxious, Danny said, not to mention dangerous. "It seems the more cents people have, the less sense they have." After Connie chewed out Harrison Ford, Danny went on, Ford flew in a few days later with a box of red wine and roses.

"To get wine and roses from Han Solo," I said with a restrained laugh, "must have been something."

"Oh no," Danny said in utter seriousness, "she wouldn't take it. She can't be bought. No one is privileged in the wilderness. It's the great equalizer."

But was it? I thought about the bloody trek through the ghost trees with Myron and my father, the trail burning up my toes and heels, the snags snagging my shins, and the new word: *stob*, meaning a broken tree branch, meaning stob in my thigh. I recalled the exhaustion in my father's eyes, angles of his face reflecting the crevasses and peaks of the mountains in the fading light, remembered Myron springing up, jumping down, gathering firewood with all the power of Moose Creek because he was fit and a relatively young man, and I didn't know if I agreed with Danny—*wilderness is the great equalizer*. Still, I glimpsed what he was saying. We were all vulnerable out there, and human vulnerability was part of the value of wilderness.

We left Connie's door, and Danny said in a whisper, "You know, Connie brings fresh tomatoes from her garden whenever she comes, and she can eat a whole plate for dinner, big ole plate like so"—he stretched his hands into a large circle—"and that's all she'll have." As he talked, Connie took on a gathering power. Where did her power come from? She seemed to be knowledgeable about the forest, have a can-do attitude, a certain grace, a strong voice, except even before I met her, I sensed her power was psychological, or spiritual, too. What was it?

Danny and I tromped around the station and the compound all afternoon, where he pulled radios out of drawers and pushed buttons and turned dials, flipped open notebooks and logbooks, had me drag huge PVC sprinklers around the grounds—the grass had to be watered as a fire barrier—and pointed out varieties of pine trees. Everything seemed big and foreign, old fashioned and elegant. He went through his tutorial quickly and by rote, and though I was frantically scribbling everything down, I felt I would never remember what to do. When he asked if I understood and I said no, he grew stern. He was no teacher, he informed me, and I was no student. I was the volunteer. Before I could respond he said, "I'm going back up to clean the attic" and shuffled over to the stairs, donning his gloves and mask. "Bats roost up there. I've been putting this off. They probably don't have bats where you work."

"I can help," I offered, though I didn't want to go up in the attic with him. The distance between what people say and what they mean is sometimes great.

"Nah," he said, already half out of the room. "It's full of guano. That's bat shit to you, professor." Our eyes met. He smiled, and I smiled back.

17 Coffin

My notebook entry, August 5, 2005: *Martin Moe, bachelor, trapper. Martin Moe sat in jail in Elk City, Idaho, the winter of 1909, suspected of murdering his partner, a man named George Archer.*

Henry Pettibone, bachelor, trapper, diarist. Pettibone ordered a coffin to be built in the fall of 1923 out of wood he'd whipsawed himself.

Danny left the station the day after I arrived. We'd both risen before dawn and I met him behind the barn, watched as he talked to Kelly, his mule, packed up, and tipped his hat as he left. And then, with the sun coming up over the airfield, I had the whole place to myself. Immediately, I started pawing through the office stacked with documents, though I was apprehensive about doing so without explicit permission. I had no idea what I was looking for, but I was enough of an archivist to know how to search. I had always been compelled by the quirky, the strange, the mysterious, the coincidental, the underside of history—those were the stories that filled my notebooks no matter what I was researching. In a fat folder in the office I found a photocopy of Henry Pettibone's diary from 1913, and another marked *Reminiscences*. I sat cross-legged on the floor conjuring up the homesteaders of the early 1900s. This was the shell, the container, into which my grandfather had come. These were the men he'd lived with.

Now, I look back on that summer at Moose Creek and understand it, at least partly, in the context of the ancestral work of constellation theory that I learned from the women at the retreat center on Cortes Island. "Constellation work is oracular," Jill, the facilitator, had said. You have to empty yourself, be careful not to control the outcome, not to want this or that to happen. Constellation only works if you respond to what's unfolding in the moment. Sometimes, the story you find isn't the story you seek. Some constellations go back a thousand years. Some involve whole communities.

Henry Pettibone, who homesteaded in the Bitterroots in 1905, was the center of a community of virile white men settling a wilderness served by doting wives whose lives were invisible. At least that's the image I had carried with me into Moose Creek, but the array of diaries, logbooks, and personal histories spread on the floor told me my academic stereotypes were worthless. Pettibone made barrels of kraut, stretched cougar hides,

Three Forks Ranger Station, formerly Shissler Cabin, 1913. Ed Gilroy photo. Courtesy of Dick Walker Historic Photo Collection.

split wood, sawed logs, made cedar shakes, bought Indian horses, shoed those horses, sewed harnesses, built fences, salted cattle, sorted vegetables, and cared for his mentally disabled brother, Rufus, with whom he lived. No wives were involved. A photo of the two brothers showed them listing to one side, their barn listing too, a world tilted toward the unusual. People cycled through the Pettibone place, including Martin Moe, the bachelor-trapper about whom not much is known. The oracle I heard in those archives told me Pettibone cared for Rufus and Moe as a mother would.

⚘

Esther had written in her *Memoirs*: "George built an airstrip below the station and a dwelling for the ranger and his family. I was privileged to be the first to inhabit the dwelling in what was to become a nationally recognized Wilderness Area."

After a day of scouring the papers in the station office, I shuffled over to the dwelling and descended to the basement looking for something, anything, of Esther. This was not the intimate, creative basement like the one in my parents' Spokane Valley home, where my mother keeps her long-arm sewing machine and my father watches TV with his dog on his lap. The dwelling basement smelled muddied, aged, and seemed as unfathomable as the unconscious. Mason jars on a shelf covered in dust; wood stove the color of a human liver; stone walls that disappeared into the dark. I puzzled over the large grate in the ceiling, then realized the grate was a throughway, heating the entire home in winter, cooling it in summer. The basement breathed.

Esther's St. Maries house didn't have a basement but there was a shed near her garden filled with rusty axes; shovels; spades; cracked ceramic pots; long, narrow wooden boxes like mini-coffins breaking apart. The shed was the only place on her property I didn't want to go, had no desire to explore. I avoided the shed with its fusty air, its eroded hinges that screamed when you opened the door, its splintered objects. It had the feel of lawlessness, violation. The basement in the dwelling wasn't the shed, but it had a shed feeling.

Some of the stories in the archives had a shed feeling, too, splintering apart as I tried to piece them together, cracking under the pressures of time. Harry Shissler, one of the earliest settlers, was Chinese or he was a white man or he was half-white and half-Chinese. He came to Selway country in 1899 because he had killed several people and robbed gold mine sluice boxes in Elk City, or he had killed one man in a bar fight in Stites. He built a cabin on the east fork of Moose Creek and nailed an elk skull and crossbones over the doorframe to scare people. His brothers joined him or they didn't. He tried running a cattle ranch, but during one of the drought years, the cattle starved, and he left. Harry was apprehended and jailed in Idaho or he was killed by the law in Oregon. But one thing was certain: in 1905, the abandoned Shissler cabin became one of the first Forest Service stations in the United States. Early rangers kept the skull and crossbones over the doorframe, kept the line between law and outlaw vague.

I found, to my surprise, that my grandfather had recorded some of this historical information himself. Just as he recorded the landscape in film, he had kept a list of place names and the stories attached to them. There I read how Martin Moe came to the Bitterroots to run traplines in the early 1900s. He was from Norway or Sweden or he wasn't. He settled on Running Creek, built a cabin, cleared land.

Moe, a bachelor, preferred working his traplines alone.

✿

Although I was alone at the station and in the dwelling for days after Danny left—I hadn't spent that much time by myself in years—I kept busy moving hoses, listening for fire weather, watching the mountains, and, of course, opening drawers and cabinets looking for past lives. I had the idea that even if Esther didn't want to remember Moose Creek, it remembered her. The logs that formed the buildings had recently been living trees and were witness to what I could never retrieve through historical records.

I saw my grandmother dancing through the dwelling, the station, the airfield, her gait unmistakable: head slightly cocked and shoulders back, moving elegantly, like a deer. My mother, I recalled, had a photo of Esther hanging clothes on a line and wearing a black-and-white checked shirt tied at the waist. Her arms outstretched, delicate and strong. "I was beautiful and I didn't know it," she said once when I showed it to her, laughing. Her laugh was sudden and unruly, exploding in a spurt with a quick hand to her mouth, because she often chuckled at what others considered impolite.

I saw Esther at Moose Creek before the area was nationally recognized, her highs and her lows, how she took in the whole land, opening her heart in a way she never had, how George promised her horses and a garden and freedom, then saw her big bellied and heavy, and then with children underfoot. I felt her eyeing the men who shuttled in and out of the station, who weren't strapped down with childcare. I saw her apron covered in flour, on her hands and knees in her garden, or in the kitchen on a hot summer day trying to cut through the chill of her marriage.

Mornings and evenings I sat on the porch with coffee and oatmeal or wine and soup, a wide view of the airfield and the deer wandering in from the forest edges, contemplating the stories I was reading by day. Although Martin Moe preferred trapping alone, for some unknown reason, he took a partner named George Archer. I envisioned Moe and Archer reading the magic of tracks along the creeks and streams, mink and marten prints, raccoon and beaver, sometimes a coyote or bear, in the trail tread of spring, the road dust of summer, the mud of fall. But they could only fully read the land after the first skiff of snow fell.

I pictured the night in January 1899 when Archer followed his traplines on skis during a blizzard and disappeared into the white. Archer's dog limped into Martin Moe's cabin wrapped in an icicle coat. Moe had a campfire, tried to still the dog, but he howled and whined, would not be calmed. At first dawn, Moe and the dog set out in search of Archer, winding their way to Pettibone's place. Pettibone organized a search and rescue, men following Archer's tracks until the tracks disappeared under another layer of snow. I followed Martin Moe and the dog on a trail out to the Bitterroot Valley, where the sheriff, the shop owners, and the hotel clerk at Elk City raised their eyebrows and their guns.

"Moe's appearance without his partner excited suspicion," my grandfather wrote. And they locked him in jail.

⌀

In the dwelling, it took me several days to explore the upstairs. A bedroom, a bathroom with working toilet, cupboards, and alcoves. I spotted a crawl space running along the roofline. Though many people had occupied this dwelling since Esther, I thought she might have stashed something—old photos, a journal, secret documents, or recipes—that those who didn't know what they were looking for might never notice. One piece of the plywood wall was held with a small finishing nail. I pried it loose one day and slipped in, scooting along the eaves and feeling into the corners. I was in her attic again as a girl feeling my way through history. But I turned up nothing except a sliver in my knee.

The summer after Archer went missing, a Nimíipuu woman was filling a basket with huckleberries while her son splashed in the shallows at Running Creek. The son spotted a hat. A gun, at least I imagined the scene that way. Then, his bare foot landed on a spine, a skull, a femur, bones purified by water and blanched by sun. Archer. The bones were collected and brought to authorities in town. People came, investigated. Archer, they conjectured, had run over a bluff on his skis and landed in a tree. He must have been alive for some time, signaling to Martin Moe, because he'd fired all of the shells from his gun. He died somewhere between the treetop and the creek.

When Martin Moe, released from jail, resumed trapping the following winter, he started to lose his mind, according to one account I read, though the details about his illness were vague. He may have spent some time in the state mental hospital in Orofino, but he then made his way back to the Bitterroots, probably the only place he felt at home. People reported seeing him wandering the mountaintops alone, a ghostly figure.

As I sifted through documents, I sometimes shivered under the layered stories. Located south of Moose Creek Ranger Station, Archer Mountain wasn't visible to me. But I read about the mahogany cross erected for the man and carved with the phrase, "Look before you leap." Grim Forest Service humor.

⚘

The ground floor of the dwelling, where I spent most of my time, had plank flooring, a braided rug in browns and beiges, a rocking chair, a kitchen stove from the 1950s, someone's amateur painting on the wall, a

crocheted blanket on the sofa, a red gingham tablecloth, a sideboard filled
with papers, haphazardly stacked. Someone had compiled a botany, glued
specimens to sheets of paper and described them:

> Queen's Cup or Bride's Bonnet, the flower is a broad bell with
>   six petals blooming on a short, leafless stalk that grows from
>   a cluster of 2 or 3 oblong, shiny leaves and a lustrous deep
>   blueberry.
> Larkspur, 6–24 inches tall, devilish lavender flowers. Poisonous to
>   cattle.
> Meadow Rue, soft, thin leaves and flower in open, branched clus-
>   ters. Rue: a sense of regret.

Sixty years since Esther had moved between these walls. Sometimes
I could smell regret in the dwelling's clammy scent, like ripe fruit, and
sometimes the ripeness signaled hope of completion. As much as Esther
said she had been miserable, the place seemed like the fruiting of a marriage and of her young womanhood. I kept searching for signs. The kitchen
cupboards were filled with canned corn and noodles, the hall drawers
with linens for firefighters and trail crews who used the place from time
to time. The small bedroom housed an iron bed and wood dresser. Atop
the dresser sat a deer's antlers—backcountry décor.

As I fingered the antlers' corrugated surface the memory of a cribbage
board Esther had owned gumshoed into my head. Someone had flattened one side of it and carved tiny holes to make the board. The hands
that forged it were skillful because the holes were perfectly aligned and
uniform, except there was something wild about it. The craftsman had left
hair clinging to the knobby end where it had been pulled from the elk's
head. Sometimes Esther seemed almost cavalier in the way she gave away
or sent to the thrift store her possessions, whatever crossed the threshold
of her house. But she cherished the elk cribbage board, kept it close like a
reminder of something good. As the days passed, I felt more and more as
if she had loved Moose Creek, despite regrets, despite loneliness, even if
that love was melancholic, creative, brooding.

George's presence, too, was moving through the place. Henry Pettibone recorded visits from Martin Moe in 1913 and 1914, but he never

wrote more than a line or two. Pettibone's diary frustrated me. Though a rich source of daily activities, it was such a utilitarian account, not much more than a to-do list, I couldn't tell how he felt about people, animals, or the land. I turned to other sources and read between the lines. I learned that Martin Moe was denied the title to the homestead on Running Creek because he was an immigrant and without citizenship, and he eventually left the Selway-Bitterroot.

Pettibone, it seemed, couldn't imagine such a fate. In 1923, in perfect health, he asked a man to build him a coffin and pointed to a pile of lumber he'd whipsawed for just that purpose. Nothing in the archives indicated what kind of lumber the coffin was made from—I imagined local western red cedar—or how it was created. Having watched my carpenter brother in his shop, I assumed there was a good amount of hand planing. Wax may have been rubbed into the box, possibly by Pettibone himself, until the cedar gleamed with rekindled life. And then it sat in the barn, unused.

A few years later, Pettibone froze his toes in a freak accident, a dire situation for someone who suffered from diabetes, and he was carted out of the wilderness. Five years after that, when he was on the edge of death, he insisted on returning. I didn't learn how Pettibone made it back to the Selway-Bitterroot in such poor health. One account claimed he hitched a ride with a backcountry pilot. In any case, his return was a more powerful statement than all his diary entries combined. What really sent a shock of emotion up my spine was discovering that my grandfather preached at the service and buried Pettibone on his wilderness homestead in the coffin he'd lovingly ordered years before. George's role in Pettibone's departure from this world felt so understated and deep with quiet love that from the moment I learned about it, I resolved to reconsider this ancestor whom to that point I had all but demonized.

18 Sitka

"There's a little camp spot just above the old bridge," Dick told me once. "The king post truss bridge first crossed North Moose there, near George's homestead cabin footings. I flew in there one fall."

We were at Dick's house watching the rain in the valley. He was talking about one of his favorite dogs, a malamute named Sitka. Dick was proud of the animal's pedigree, part wolf and a relative of the dogs

Sitka, Upper Selway, 1969. Dick Walker photo.

used by the Tenth Mountain Division in World War II. Sitka had hiked over a thousand miles with Dick through the Anaconda-Pintler and the Selway-Bitterroot Wildernesses.

"I remember that night, Sitka, he went around and around and around, trying to get comfortable, to bed down for the night. We finally went to sleep, and then the next morning his whole rear end was shot, his hips were bothering him tremendously. We got up, and we went up on a little mound there. There were a lot of cow elk there and some calves. A lot of barking. Sitka was aware, but he was having a hard time focusing, and he was really hurting. We went back into the woods there, and I let him sniff around, and I guess that's where I finally decided that this was where he deserved to go to rest. He was happily sniffing, and I dispatched him there, and let him lie."

Dick's story of Sitka has stayed with me for years. The tenderness of it.

"I went back every spring thereafter," Dick said. "And the dog just melded into the ground until there was no more Sitka. Oh, he was there, but he was part of a thousand different living things."

The summer I lived with Esther, she kept telling me, not in words but in everything we did, that recycling was holy, reusing a way to wholeness.

19 Voices

Each morning the summer I volunteered at Moose Creek, after boiling coffee, I checked in over the radio and listened for fire weather. A male voice ruffled by static would say something like: "One and a half miles northwest of Fish Lake airstrip, twenty acres, eastern exposure, moderate speed, upper one-third of the slope, heavy fuels, wind speed light out of the west, white smoke, active torching," and I'd jot it in a notebook. Then I'd head outside. The strip beside the airfield holds six large campsites complete with picnic tables, fire pits, and a community outhouse.

Another duty was visiting the campsites, or, as the manual instructed:

> You will greet hikers, stock users, boaters, outfitters, pilots, anglers, hunters, and research field scientists. All have a stake in the Wilderness at Moose Creek. Many have been visiting Moose Creek area for 30–40 years; or their parents or grandparents were associated with it.

The people I met came to connect with the wilderness, to be in a place bigger than the big places they were from, cities mostly. I remember a young man who liked to kill squirrels—"tree rats"—with his .22 rifle; a family group from England who had some connection to Moose Creek; a former ranger who flew in with his wife for their fiftieth wedding anniversary; three hippies from California, one who cruised the place barefoot, who said barefoot was the only way to feel Earth, and asked to use the Singer treadle machine to mend his shirt; a dentist from Colorado who brought in Pabst Blue Ribbon and asked me to go for a ride in his airplane (I didn't). And of course, there was Joe. Joe made appearances,

Amy riding Lily the mule, Selway-Bitterroot Wilderness, 2019. DJ Lee photo.

transporting fishermen and hikers, even giving flying lessons to a guy from Missoula.

The day after Danny left, I strolled down the airstrip in my Moose Creek Ranger District T-shirt, as if the shirt could magically bestow wilderness expertise on its wearer. Everything was heightened. I was scared I would screw up. Greeting people was one thing. How to address their diffuse problems was something else.

A few campsites were occupied by tents and airplanes—as odd as it seems for a wilderness, the sites are large enough to park an airplane—but no people were around, all out hiking or fishing. At the end of the strip, the very last campsite, I heard acid rock blasting, and as I approached, a stout, top-heavy man with skinny legs flounced out of the woods wearing a T-shirt that read: "I have a PHD, Pretty Hard Dick." I noticed a pistol hung from his belt.

I commented on the boom box attached to a solar panel.

"Gotta have my tunes," he said as if we were like-minded concert pals, and he shook my hand.

"Some of the campers might want it quieter," I pointed out. And some of the animals, I thought. He grinned, a wide mouth and small teeth, and turned down the music. I was relieved and then alarmed as I noticed a dead snake, diamonds studded across its back like the data of temptation. It was draped across a log next to the boom box.

The man, whose name was Chester, said he'd rafted down the Selway River with his two young sons, who popped out of the tent just then, blond and shirtless and covered in a fine dust. Chester said he and his boys had come down from Paradise Creek, fifty miles upriver. They'd capsized and the boat sucked the younger of his two under. I was taking a good look around the camp and did note an inflatable rubber raft a few yards away lying in the dirt. Very small for three people.

I asked if he'd killed the snake.

"Yes ma'am," he said in a seductive voice, and I noted that though he was strange and off-kilter, he had a kind of bad-boy charm. The snake had been crawling around and scaring his boys and he was going to roast it for a snack. I got a whiff of his acrid stench as he spoke—he obviously hadn't bathed in days. Shooting a snake wasn't against the law, but it struck me as an excessive gesture in the campground.

From a plastic sleeve, Chester removed a map and spread it on the ground. "Do you know where the graves are?" he asked. I wasn't aware of any graves. "Some guys in the 1890s," he said. They were bandits, and that's what had piqued Chester's interest.

One of the men, Shean, was a forty-seven-year-old Irishman and the other, Eddie Wheeler, a wanderer and ne'er-do-well from Connecticut. A third man, Printz, was a shadowy fellow. Printz lived to tell the story. A friend of Chester's had come across the graves story in a typewritten script and the two men had discussed it, apparently with much enthusiasm. I wouldn't have believed Chester, but sure enough, there on the map, a marker read *Graves* on an area labeled *Deadmam Flats*, a spot right next to the place where George's original homestead was to have been.

How fortuitous. This curious little man is his own archive. I asked about the banditry.

They were horse thieves, Chester informed me, stole some ponies from the Nimíipuu on the Camas Prairie near Weippe. According to the story he'd read, they left for the mountains in August 1894 and built a cabin at the confluence of East Moose and North Moose Creeks. They intended to strike it rich prospecting for gold, but when winter came, they started trapping marten and mink, which brought five dollars per hide.

Chester believed they got along fine, piling up the furs, dreaming of the money they'd make in the spring. "It pains me to think about it," he said, "because there never was any gold back here." The bandits were banking on a commodity the land didn't produce instead of what it was famous for—treacherous terrain and biting winters. That winter happened to be one of the harshest, he recalled reading. Shean and Wheeler both took sick. Shean couldn't catch his breath and Wheeler lost his eyesight along with his mind. A number of cursed illnesses could have beset the men. Shean died and Wheeler moved outside the cabin, where he wandered in the cold without a hat or coat, crying, I been traveling all night; I'm hungry. Can I stay here the night and get something to eat?

Chester quoted the line with a smile on his face and a frown in his voice.

I asked if the ghosts and graves would spook his sons as the rattler had.

He buckled his heavy upper body in a shrug and said it didn't matter. He lived by the principle, which he was teaching them, that it was better for a person to look back and regret the things they did and not the things they didn't do.

He folded his map and called his boys to get their shoes on.

From Chester's camp, I proceeded down the airfield to its end and started hiking down, eyes to the ground as I navigated between razor-sharp rocks and the sticks, bundles of needles, leaves, tumbled pebbles, and cones on the path.

Another man, balding with a stubbly gray beard, was coming up as I was going down. I stopped to let him pass and we exchanged greetings.

"Flew in this morning," he said. He was of medium build and not out of proportion like Chester. "I'm not at the campsites. I set up back in the woods." He rubbed his forehead with his soft, manicured hand. He was an anesthesiologist from Washington State. Friends had been telling him about Moose Creek for years. "I finally came, and I love it."

He'd just been swimming at the beach where Moose Creek and the Selway River come together, and he encouraged me to do the same. "Confluences are pretty special places," he said, and he launched into a lecture about their meaning. They were places where diverse cultures met, traded, and shared traditions. "Think of the confluence of the Missouri and the Mississippi," he said, "flowing right through the heart of St. Louis." He discoursed for several minutes in vague and general terms about the significance confluences held for Indigenous people.

Confluences. I probably recall these men so vividly because they typified two kinds of people I've encountered throughout my years in the Bitterroots. The unpretentious rogue with a taste for history and the refined professional on a quest for meaning. We parted and I made it to the white beach. It was scattered with driftwood, framed with wild willows, alive with spiders, ants, dragonflies, and bees. The beach drew to a point where the two waters joined and ruffled up in splashes of white. I hadn't planned to swim, but it was hot out. I waded knee-deep into the turbid water, cold cutting into my bones.

⊕

Humanity continued to crackle through the radio every morning. The urgent, whipping voice reporting fire weather and those of fire patrol pilots, Forest Service dispatchers, and lookouts.

But the voice I listened for was Connie's.

Every summer, Connie recruited teams of Iowa high school farm kids to do trail maintenance. Over the next month, her voice sizzled on the radio from all over: "We're up on Snake Ridge," she would say, before her voice disintegrated into pops and scratches and cosmic static and silence. At times, I believed I hadn't heard her at all.

Because she was deep in the woods, I had to relay her whereabouts to dispatchers in the front country, let them know she was okay. Hearing her meant she was alive.

One morning, I completed my chores, and when I came back to the station, the door to Connie's room was ajar. An invitation? No. Yes. I stood, back pressed against the doorjamb, sliding my eye along the crack. A single mattress covered with a patchwork quilt was in full view. Next to it, a night table held a white gas lantern and a pile of books. I squinted. If I could see the books, I would know Connie. If we were drawn to the same author, we would be relatives. At the time I was reading William Faulkner's *The Sound and the Fury*, the poetry of William Blake, and Alice Munro's *View from Castle Rock*. Connie's titles scrambled and blurred before me. I inched my head into the crack, and the door squawked open a foot.

I got a whiff of old earthiness and the familiar feeling of acting a narrative of my own making as it was unfolding, except this time I had the pressure of being inside my grandparents' story. On the far side of the room, several headlamps hung from a nail. A fleece jacket lay across the bed, limp, but as if her body had recently warmed it. Several bottles of red wine were lined up in a neat row against the wall. I leaned in farther, and then my foot was across the threshold. Not an invitation. I was breaking and now entering.

A stack of notecards bearing a photo of a pileated woodpecker sat next to the books. I kneeled by the bedside, scribbling the titles into my journal—Barbara Kingsolver's *Small Wonder*, John McPhee's *Coming into the Country*, E. M. Forster's *A Passage to India*, and—I felt a swell of recognition—Alice Munro's *Runaway*. Connie was reading Munro!

The door swung wide. A young man straddled the arch, dirt covering his jeans, glowering at me from under a brown felt hat. He didn't look like a camper but like he owned the place.

I stood up, startled. "Hi!"

He left the doorway without a word.

Out the window I could see him unloading stock and hauling gear into the station. Danny had said something about mule packers. Where he came from mystified me. Who was he? How long was he going to stay? I had one towering fear. He'd report me for being in Connie's room and send me away just when I was starting to feel comfortable in the place.

I heard pots and pans banging in the kitchen. I would confess. I would say that my curiosity got the best of me.

I found him boiling water and making a sandwich. "I'm the volunteer," I said.

"I know who you are." He wiped his hands on a towel and told me he was the Moose Creek mule packer. "I'm Gabe. I was supposed to be here

a few days ago. Had to haul some supplies to Connie. I usually come in
Tuesdays and leave Thursdays."

"I see." He spread peanut butter on bread while I leaned against the
end of the counter.

"You probably wondered what I was doing." I told him I was sorry,
mentioned my grandparents, said I'd been looking for historical materials,
between doing my chores and meeting campers and pilots, of course. I
may have used the phrase *wilderness pioneer.*

He squatted to check the stove flame—he was heating soup—and
turned the dial higher. "There's some stuff in the office."

"I noticed," I said cautiously.

"There's a lot of shit in there, brooms and mops and what-not. There's
papers, too, and a black binder with a bunch of old clippings. Handwrit-
ten pages from like—I don't know—nineteen-ten." He pulled some mugs
from the cabinet. "I was a history major in college."

Gabe poured us each a cup of coffee and then told me more about his
college experience. He was a graduate of Montana State University where
he'd taken English and French literature in addition to American history; he'd spent time at a ranch near West Yellowstone, where he guided
famous people on hunting, fishing, and hiking trips—Supreme Court
justices, movie stars, professional athletes. He preferred Moose Creek to
West Yellowstone. "Here, people take wilderness seriously," he said in a
crisp voice.

"Like Harrison Ford?" I said.

He smiled.

Gabe. A mix of old and new West, he would eventually become
the ranch manager for a famous media mogul who had an expansive
spread in Montana. Buy expensive horses and hire someone else to
pack mules and make lunch. I wasn't surprised when I heard about it
later. Gabe was a real cowboy. But you could see his glittery side even
at Moose Creek.

Gabe and I worked companionably over the next days. I visited campers, dragged hoses and watered grass, kept track of airplane landings. He
fed mules, piled slash behind the station, mowed the airfield with an
old-fashioned cutting blade hitched to a mule team, hauled supplies up
to the Shissler Peak lookout, and split wood. Then he left, taking my let-

ters to Myron and Steph and my mother. He also was the Moose Creek postman.

After that, I felt free to keep diving into the papers in the office. The office became my gateway to understanding the wilderness, if such a thing was possible. One definition of *wilderness*—as the sign on the wall of the station quoting the Wilderness Act plainly states—is a place "untrammeled by man," but the archives proved the land was deeply trammeled by human lives and dreams.

Strangely, I often found that stories I read in the office one day were reenacted in the wilderness the next, like the man who went blind fighting fire in the 1890s.

One morning on a day Gabe was gone from the station, Connie's voice echoed over the radio: "We were going to finish the trail to Elk Summit, but we're turning back now because of fire."

"Copy," I said.

"They've got the station wrapped"—covered in fireproof foil so that it looked like a meatloaf in a cafeteria. She told me her location and plans for the day, her voice panicked.

I jotted them down, and then I reached out over the airwaves. "I hope to meet you," I said. Silence stretched long enough for me to wish I hadn't said it.

Her voice sounded again. "I don't know when we'll be out of here." Another silence. Then: "I hope to meet you too."

The exchange felt so intimate. It wasn't until I walked out of the station and stood on that pelvic plateau that I understood that my solitude, my need for companionship, had blinded me to my unremarkable place in this vast landscape. In the midst of a raging fire and with a crew of Iowa farm kids to tend to, meeting me was the least of her concerns.

⌀

Even in her absence, Connie was an ever-shifting story. Someone stopped by the station every few days asking about her. Two hikers, young men not over twenty, had met Connie by chance at a restaurant in Missoula. They'd shared a table next to her and she struck up a conversation about the Selway-Bitterroot. Her description was so enticing, they set out on a fifty-mile backpack and had arrived at the station a hot mess, reeking of body odor and on an alpine high, asking for Connie. Nearly every old-timer—pilots and hikers and people on horseback who visited Moose Creek year after year—wanted to see Connie. When I said, "I don't know when she'll be here," they presented me with a laundry list of things that needed to be fixed. What was she going to do about the shingles on the station's roof? How about the pine beetles? Were there plans to control the spotted knapweed, the invasive plant that choked out cattle and horse feed? Some people burst through the station door calling "Connie!" and their faces fell when I came around the corner.

After four weeks in the wilderness, a radio call came from the Forest Service dispatcher: "Connie won't be there to relieve you. She had a family emergency," said a woman's blunt voice. "Can you stay longer?" I was set to walk out the next day, and the request came as a gift. I had come to think of Moose Creek as home. Myron would understand. His one letter to me had said, "I'll be waiting but take your time."

A week later, Connie arrived on horseback with two fully packed mules. I had no preparation. She was just there, next to the station wearing a scarf around her neck and a cowboy hat. She had blonde hair and a pale, Scandinavian face with dainty features, so different from what I had imagined. Gabe strode over from the corral and started to unload her panniers—each one weighing fifty pounds or more. Connie's presence infused him with more energy and spunk than I'd seen so far. Tom, a tall, dark-haired, flamboyant man in his thirties who worked a fire lookout, was spending a few days at the station. He leaned against a fence post making wisecracks. Connie paid him no mind. She was more worried about putting her horse to pasture.

"No, you're not going to do that." Connie yanked a pannier from Gabe. "I can unpack my own things."

"Fine," Gabe said, wiping his hands on his jeans.

She was sixty-three and didn't stoop. She gave the impression of someone confident, young, and strong. She glowed.

She swooped into the kitchen, opening cupboards and drawers to spirit away the fresh vegetables and fruit she'd packed in. She'd brought wine and the newspaper. And she had news from around the forest. "The fire marshal's closing the trails out of Bear Creek," she said. "Did you see Charlie? Did he come through on his way to the Lochsa River?" She took the binoculars from the table, where I'd kept them since Danny had left, and placed them on the windowsill. She moved pots from the counter where I'd left them to dry.

She was putting the station back in order, her order.

I stood in the shadows, nervous, in awe.

"Thank you for staying so long," she said, finally turning her eyes on me. I stepped forward. "I have paperwork here for you to sign." She smiled, but not enough, no, not enough for me.

It dawned on me in that instant: Connie's arrival meant my departure, my utter separation from the wilderness. All the weeks I had waited to meet her, I hadn't quite realized her presence meant I would no longer be needed. The idea tore me apart.

The rest of the day, I folded my belongings into my backpack. I formed my shirts into long, jelly-roll shapes. Would I be able to hike out? Of course I could hike the twenty-five miles with my forty-pound pack. The weeks of working the station had put muscles on me. I squeezed toothpaste from a tube, only enough for the trip out, and wrapped that in a tiny square of cellophane. But would I be able to walk away from this life so close to the land and the connections to my ancestors?

That evening, Connie and I ate together. She poured glasses of wine and made small talk about the salad she'd prepared, about the news in the front country, and about a friend of hers exhibiting an art show.

"What fascinates me about homesteaders like your grandfather," she said, when I brought up the research I'd done in the office, "is the community, the people who carved out a place here, as hard as it was. How did they do that? We know there's been human influence here that goes back further into the past than the Nez Perce even. I think the power of this place has something to do not just with our connection to the land but to people. People speak out of the land. Even Dick Walker—who is as fierce a wilderness advocate as they come—said that to me once, *I feel the human presence here, and as much as I want wilderness to be without human influence, it cannot be.*"

She confessed her allegiances: she felt loyalty to her daughters and her husband Lloyd, ten years her senior. But she was devoted to the Bitterroots with a big love, the way that people love God or Buddha. She believed the land had taught her vital things, and she had a lot to learn.

"Before I came to the Selway-Bitterroot, I was an impatient, gung-ho kind of person, one who needed to be in control," she said as we sat at the table in dimming light.

In her first summer as a wilderness ranger, she backpacked up to Seven Lakes, high in the mountains, planning to loop back to her camp. At five thousand feet, she ran into snow, yet she would not deviate from her plan, she told me. The snow got deeper, the trail disappeared under the snow. She soldiered on. And then, she turned a corner and realized she was lost. She stopped. Her boss had told her: "If you can't find your way, go downhill until you find a stream. Follow the stream; it will come out somewhere." But at seven thousand feet, getting down was difficult. Plants grew in tangles and knots and water ran underneath the snow. Eventually she came to a place that intersected with a trail, and right there on the trail, she found a Steller's jay feather. Ash gray on one side, cobalt blue with black stripes on the other. Finding the feather made her stop, and when she stopped, she had a revelation about her character. "When I didn't know what was going on, or where to go, or what action to take, instead of panicking or trying to control things, I needed to stop, keep my wits about me, and know that I could get out," she said. "There was no way I could be in control of this place. What I needed was patience."

And so, over time, Connie had developed the patience of a moose. She felt more at home in the wild than in any other place. One of her daughters had said to her, "Isn't going to the wilderness putting your head in the sand? If you're going back there because you're an environmentalist, the real environmental problems are out here, where people are doing all these horrible things, polluting the water, the air, burning carbon like crazy. The wilderness is the last place that needs an environmentalist." Connie understood the contradiction, but the wilderness was where she had to be, where her life had meaning.

Nearing retirement, she'd become more reflective. Connecting people with land and with each other, that's how Connie saw herself. When she thought of the timeline of the Selway-Bitterroot Wilderness, she thought of drawers. "I've looked in the drawers at Moose Creek and seen names from the past, names like Bob Marshall who everyone knows. And I've seen names no one knows anything about. I've thought of my name being there some day, but as someone no one knows about."

I lit the kerosene lamp. Connie's talk and her fresh food and wine had relaxed me, and I asked her, "How did you come to Moose Creek? I mean, why did you choose this place?"

"Well," she said, leaning back in her chair, face ambering in the lamp-light, "I was teaching high school Spanish in Essex, Iowa, and somehow I signed up for a workshop called American Wilderness Leadership School. Now Iowa is one of the six states that doesn't have wilderness, so wilderness is foreign to that part of the country. Although I was a rural person—that's how I learned to love the land. But I was in this school and there was a young woman, she had been a fire lookout in the Bitter-roots. And she had taken some photographs—just some snapshots, you know—and she had those with her. She showed them to me, and I was just overwhelmed. Something went *wang* in my heart. I'd never encountered mountains like that, one after another, as far as the eye could see. I thought, I have to be in that place. I have to get there. How can I be there? So I filled out a Forest Service job application. A few months later, a guy hired me over the phone. That was twenty years ago."

Connie had first come to the wilderness as a middle-aged woman, had been so drawn to the place that it became her life. At forty-five, I wondered if the same thing would happen to me.

"I got in my dad's pickup," she continued, "and headed off by myself. I thought, Connie, what the heck are you doing? I almost turned the truck around and pulled back into my safe little home in Iowa. But I kept going. And when I saw the Bitterroots spread before me, well, I was overcome. I had a sense of connecting with something larger than myself."

I asked if hers was a common experience.

"Oh, yes," she said. "A lot of people come in here and it changes them forever."

20 Deep

October 20, 2018

Connie told me once: "My very first trip to the Selway-Bitterroot, I stopped at every bridge on Highway 12, I walked across those bridges and watched the water. When I got to the wilderness, I stopped at every pack bridge. I was in awe of everything. I crossed the bridge at Split Creek and touched a western red cedar, which I'd never seen before in my life, and it felt like angels' wings."

But tonight, at the Gedney Creek campsite, I go to bed with an axe, which I usually don't do. When all but a few embers glow from the fire pit, I head for the tent, dragging the lumberjack's favorite tool. A cottonwood rattles, the moon projects branches as playful fingers against the nylon tent. *Angels' wings.* The branches outside my tent don't feel like angels—they are menacing. Cougars, bears, and wolves creeping through the forest cross my mind, and strange people lurking in the corners.

Strange like James Dimaggio, who in 2013 abducted a teenage girl in California, shot her mother and brother, and drove to the Frank Church River of No Return Wilderness, which borders the Selway-Bitterroot to the south. The national news, which I followed with fascinated horror, focused in on "remote Idaho," chronicling how the FBI took three hours to hike a few miles through the mountains. One officer was quoted as saying, "There's nothing out there," meaning nothing human-made, as if he'd never imagined such a place. After the girl was rescued, another officer speculated that Dimaggio had had a mental breakdown, noting the incongruity of Dimaggio's taking a gray house cat deep into the wilderness.

My friend's words resurface: *I've seen some sketchy people at the Fog Mountain Trailhead.*

I've met sketchy people at trailheads, too, a boy with the hollow face who'd watched *Into the Wild* too many times and was living his own Alexander Supertramp story, carrying a thin bedroll, not a proper sleeping bag or tent, a few miles from Race Creek. When I came upon him, he was sitting on a log next to a dead squirrel and rattlesnake he'd shot with his .22, and I was shocked at how skinny and unprepared he was in his torn cotton trousers. When I offered gummy bears and trail mix from my pack, he devoured them greedily.

But the deeper into the woods you went, I knew, the more strangers seemed like family. Once I was backpacking with Steph. In shorts and strappy yoga tops, in the thick and swampy air, we padded along a trail, sweat beading on our noses, dodging an army of insects, the anticipation of reaching Fish Lake Saddle and rushing down to the cool lake driving us on. At our halfway point, Stoney Creek, Steph's cheeks were burning, her eyes glazed. We tramped on until she said, "I need to rest." We stopped, biting flies ravaging our skin, mosquitoes joining in, panic rising. I'd been rationing our water, limiting us to small sips, but I used some of our precious supply to wet a handkerchief and tie it around her neck. The flies were one scourge too many, and I silently cursed myself for putting my daughter in danger. I didn't want to show how worried I was.

And then there appeared two men on horses leading a mule team, the only people we'd encountered since a volunteer ranger in our campsite early that morning. I looked up longingly: they were dressed in long pants and long-sleeved shirts to shield themselves from the insects. The large horses were drenched with sweat, the men's faces dirty, and a musty smell filled the air. Steph, sixteen, and I stood staring into the wild, sideways eyes of the horses, angry or frightened, tails swishing.

The men had guns strapped to their belts. I studied my hiking pole, a paltry weapon—my knife was buried in my pack. An image flashed before me: my phantom self, screaming hysterically—*Leave her alone! Take me instead!*—and the men rolling their eyes and riding away.

Steph and I were already shuttled off the trail, knee-deep in a thicket of waxy-leaved bushes, when one of the men, with stubbled skin and dark shadows under his eyes, reached into his pocket for something and threw it to me.

By the time I figured out what it was—a full bottle of insect lotion—the men were gone, slipped through the ether to some cowboy dimension. I smothered Steph's skin with lotion, rubbing tenderly, and then slathered some on myself, and we hiked on, insects hovering but keeping their distance.

↢

Safe in my tent, axe by my side, I snuggle farther into the bag. Connie couldn't have encountered someone menacing because she was too deep in the woods. Deep is where people take care of one another, even if, like the cowboys, it is an act of generosity with a hint of contempt.

The bag rubs against my ear, amplifying my own breath. My feet are ice cubes. I stuff a blanket and down coat into the bottom, waiting for warmth. Something's prowling around close to my ear on the other side of the nylon. Light footsteps. Thwack of hooves. I lie perfectly still and the prowling turns to trickling water, stirring leaves.

I try to feel Connie's kindly spirit in the wind and shadows, yet all I can do is dream up the ways she might have survived. She could have crawled into a hole and covered herself with subalpine fir branches. I'd heard once of a man who slept through a storm under a curtain of subalpine fir needles. Those trees can save your life. Ace the dog could have kept her warm, alive. Or she could have encountered the cowboys with the lotion or some relative of theirs, who brought her to their camp, restored her, and were even now on their way to town.

Into the night I toss and turn, crashing between dream and dread. The hidden world often glimpsed before sleep permeates the tent. Finding it impossible to engage my rational mind, I click on my headlamp and run out, dragging my axe and sleeping bag. Inside the car, I fold down the seats and lock the doors, but even then, I feel scattered, unsure. Because no one knows for certain about the other realm, land of pixies, sylphs, wilis, protectors of women and preservers of environments, genial wood spirits who can also be angry, especially if they did not want to die.

21 Phantom

When we were children, my father was always spiriting my brothers and me away from our rough Seattle cul-de-sac, which was flanked by low-income apartment complexes, mini-malls, freeways, skyscrapers, and street people. Money was tight. We never escaped far. Weekend trips to the North Cascades, car camping spots crisscrossed by rutted roads where we rode bicycles, roasted hotdogs in a metal fire pit, and slept in a big blue canvas tent were the norm. Though I now know how different these campgrounds are from federally protected wilderness like the Selway-Bitterroot, they felt wild to me. I often traipsed off by myself, which my parents approved of since we were far from the dangers of the city. Whenever I found a spider web strung between fir branches and trembling with dew, or a wild raspberry about to fall from its nub, I'd feel a strange pull, a desire to move beyond myself and disappear into that webbed tremble and merge with something radically other.

All grown up, my brothers and I had veered away from camping, but after Esther died and we found the Selway-Bitterroot, my father made camping his priority—our priority—pulling his adult children, their spouses, and children into a set of rigorous hikes and backpacks throughout the American West: Utah, Oregon, Washington, Arizona, California, Nevada, Wyoming, and Alaska. Maybe because we'd spent so much of our childhoods in the forests of the Pacific Northwest, we allowed ourselves to be swept up in his plans.

Then, seven years after my grandmother died, he organized a family trip to Moose Creek. Five days in the wilderness. Every member of the immediate family—sixteen in all—was present. Some hiked in, others flew in with Joe. Why the extravagance? We were there to celebrate our roots, he said. Though we are not a warring family, this was the land of our ancestors, and I expected conflict. Yet in the wilderness—the only distractions were eagles and hawks flying overhead, woodpeckers perched on snags, and fields filled with ferns and edged with paintbrush—we were able to relax. From what I remember, we swam, hiked, fished, ate, napped, and extended each day into the night around a campfire, feeling connected to the land and to one another.

That easy intimacy ended the day before we were to depart.

We'd just had lunch when our father said, "Gather round, now." He wanted us to march up to the dwelling—George and Esther's first

Moose Creek landing field and ranger station, 1936. Family photo.

home—to take a family photo. My three brothers and I stood around the empty fire pit filled with charred logs, waiting.

My mother began tossing the leftover food into the coolers with a kind of aggression I hadn't witnessed in years. She could get moody at meal-times, especially during preparation and cleanup. She seemed particularly upset now, neck muscles and jaw strung tight, avoiding eye contact. Tension tore through the campsite, through me. My brothers and I offered to help. She barked an emphatic "No!" and swished past us in her hiking khakis. I don't recall my brothers' reactions, but they probably sighed or shook their heads. I shrunk into a shell, tabled my emotions. Steph entertained the small children, while the in-laws—Myron and my brothers' wives—exchanged wry looks, as if bemused to be part of this family.

My father, who hardly ever noticed my mother's moods, clapped his hands, trying to motivate us to walk to the dwelling. "Come on!" His tone was overly jubilant, as if to break my mother's hostile silence. Nothing seemed to help.

Just then, a young woman appeared on the edge of our campsite, cheeks hollowed and brown hair chopped unevenly, startling us. A rope held up her dirty hiking shorts, and her knees were a splash of bruises, scrapes, and wounds. She looked freakish next to our pile of food and gear—jars of licorice and noodle ramen from Costco, large bowls and pans, the Coleman stove of my youth, a supersized box of Hershey bars, and several ice chests full of rib-eye steak, fillet of salmon, a watermelon, berries, salad mix, and the ingredients for homemade ice cream with a hand-crank machine. Five large tents stood among the trees, one for each of my brothers' families, one for my parents, and one for Myron, Steph, and me.

"I heard you know Joe," the young woman said, her voice tight and clenched, as if choking back tears. She looked to be about twenty. "I talked to the ranger, and he said you know Joe."

"We know him," my mother said, placing a package of hotdog buns on the table, eyeing our visitor warily.

"I saw him a couple of days ago," the woman said. "He was dropping off some fishermen or something. I was asking him for a ride, and he said he'd fly me out with you guys." She cleared her throat. "Can you tell him I'm fine. I'm walking out."

"It's twenty-five miles to the nearest road," my mother said gently, the woman's neediness having shaken her out of her mood.

At this, the woman's body arched and sank, breath-like. Then she started quivering. She was definitely not okay. My mother threw her arms around the woman, who howled loudly at her touch.

"What's wrong?" my mother said, stepping back with her arm still on the woman's shoulder.

"I've been hiking three months straight," the woman managed to croak through tears. "Six hundred miles. And we're only halfway."

We? I had assumed she was alone and somehow abandoned in the woods. Her hike now sounded intentional, though unintentionally self-destructive. I panned the scene, my brothers' faces and those of my sisters-in-law, Myron, and my father, who watched in silence. Everyone, in fact, wore a mute, stony expression. Even the children had gone quiet.

Then I noticed a man standing behind a Douglas fir on the edge of the camp not far from the outhouse. Bushy beard, dirt streaked down his hiking pants. At first he seemed cowardly, with his lowered eyelids, and I thought he'd forced the woman to come to our camp, using our mutual acquaintance with Joe as an excuse to ask for something. But the more I studied him, the more intently he fixed a menacing glare on my mother. The sight of her holding the woman seemed to be infuriating him.

"How much weight have you lost?" my mother said.

The woman meticulously unknotted the rope and pulled out her pants to show three or four inches of fabric stretching beyond her jagged hips and concave belly. She seemed so fragile and vulnerable next to the sturdy trees, next to our sprawling family, our mountains of food, next to the man by the tree. "These were tight on me when I left. I don't know if I can go on, and he's so mad at me."

"Who?" My mother turned and locked eyes with the bearded man.

"My boyfriend—we're hiking the Centennial Trail."

Trails, I'd learned by then, are classified in expedition guides as easy, intermediate, and difficult. Long-distance trails are their own species, like the 2,200-mile Appalachian Trail from Georgia to Maine, the 2,660-mile Pacific Coast Trail from California to Washington State, the 3,100-mile Continental Divide Trail from New Mexico to Idaho, and the Centennial, which travels north through Idaho from Nevada to Canada. Though on the shorter side at 1,200 miles, the Centennial is among the most difficult, with dramatic elevation changes, where the ground transforms underfoot from high-desert shrub steppe to low dry hills, old burns, alpine meadows, basalt and granite spires, undammed rivers, and glacier-fed lakes. The trail passes through some of the most remote wilderness country in the United States, like the Selway-Bitterroot. Other long trails regularly skirt towns and settlements, but resupply towns on the Centennial can be six hundred miles apart.

"It took a year of planning. I have to finish," the woman said. "It's our dream." She was saying the words, yet they sounded blank, like a dream she no longer remembered.

My mother kept patting her back. I was astonished at how she calmed the woman, and how the woman calmed her, as if they had found in one another exactly what they needed. "Is this your dream or his?" she asked the woman in a tone so frank it made me wince. The woman seemed to crumple into her. My mother continued whispering comfort, and then she spoke with authority. "You need something to eat. You need some chocolate!" She led the woman by the hand to the picnic table and gave her several Hershey bars. "You know," she said as the woman peeled back the wrapper, "your dream can end here. If he's any kind of man, he'll understand."

I looked for the man. He was gone.

"Give Joe my message," the woman said after she'd eaten the chocolate in a few large gulps. "Tell him I'm sorry." She seemed to float toward our grandparents' dwelling. We stood mesmerized, following her with our eyes until she became a pinprick against the forest.

My father herded us up the airstrip to the ranger's dwelling. Once there, he pulled out of his side bag a bundle of white T-shirts, each with a map of the station printed on the front. One shirt for each of us, even the little children. He'd been meticulous at guessing the sizes, and like the dutiful children we were, we slipped them on and posed for a photo. I remember thinking we looked like a religious sect, and in a sense we were—devoted to family even as we sometimes resisted.

After the photo, everyone dispersed. My mother climbed the stairs and stood beside me on the porch. The sky was stretched tight and wide across the plateau that day, the mountain straight in front of us, Grizzly

Saddle, a dozen different colors of orange. "Sometime in the mid-nineteen thirties, Mother got news that one of her sisters was sick," my mother said in a soft, remembering tone, "so she got on a horse and rode toward Kooskia. She was traveling alone on a patch of trail where the tread was worn and dropped off into a deep ravine, so she got off the horse to lead it across. Just as she was about to step, she saw a rattlesnake coiled and ready to strike. There she was between a five-hundred-pound animal, a precipice, and a rattler."

"Then what?" I asked.

"I think she was able to grab a branch and flick the snake over the edge, but Mother always called that a moment of reckoning, when she realized she really was out in the middle of nowhere. I remember her saying that one thought went through her head: What in the world am I doing here all by myself?"

I, of course, thought of the young woman we'd just met, her parallel to Esther. *Moose Creek Ranger Station, in the Selway-Bitterroot Wilderness, where I spent many miserable years married to a man I didn't love and who didn't love me.* And in that moment, I noticed someone lounging against a support beam on the porch a few feet away, sun falling on his closed eyelids. It took me a minute to recognize him, but this was the surly man from before, the distressed woman's boyfriend. Black curly hair matted to his head, beard the size of a Victorian patriarch's.

My mother's eyes followed mine, and within seconds she was kneeling beside him. My mother was like that—a whirlwind, fast moving, fast thinking. She looked into his face, urging him and the woman to join us for dinner. "We have some nice big steaks and salmon and vegetables. She needs something to eat. She can't make it much farther without nourishment."

The boyfriend said nothing, and my mother stood up, but he kept his eyes, beady as bullets, on us as we left to join the rest of the family who were at the corral petting the mules and horses.

That night, we barbecued and my mother set out salad and fruit. Neither the woman nor her boyfriend showed up, but they were there because we rehearsed the incident again and again, turning it, rather than the story of our grandparents, into the story that bound our family.

"Tragic," one of my brothers said, and we all nodded.

"What'll happen to her?" Steph asked.

"There's no way she'll be able to walk out in her condition. What women do to their bodies because of men," my mother said, and I was surprised because she normally didn't make such strong statements about gender, especially in front of my brothers. There were volunteers at the ranger station, she went on, who might be able to persuade the woman to get help. "I hope she ditches him."

My father shook his head and said in a loud, combative voice that if he would've thought quickly enough, he would have kicked the crap out of that boyfriend. His bravado did little to change the mood.

My mother set plates on the table next to the crackling fire, and we dished up, but we didn't eat. We just stared into our food in collective shock. Afterward, she and I wrapped the leftovers while listening to the stridulating crickets, the low scraping ache they released into the night.

❦

The day of our departure, my father had us up and packed, sleeping bags and tents rolled up, food in boxes, everything ordered and organized by 6 a.m. The only morning person among us, he scurried around inspecting us as if we were in the military. At 6:30 on the dot, Joe's plane sputtered to a stop on the airfield and we hurried over with armfuls of gear. During the summer months, flights in and out of Moose Creek take place in the morning hours when the air is thick. Hot air is thin air, and thin air makes it more difficult for planes to lift and land safely. Over the next few hours, Joe made five trips to and from Hamilton to accommodate all sixteen of us and our gear. Each time, he strapped three or four of us into the airplane seats, made sure the weight was balanced, and shut the doors.

Somehow it came about that my mother and I were the last two left at camp, I suppose because we had taken it upon ourselves to clean up, stacking leftover wood in a neat pile near the fire ring, taking down the clothesline we'd strung between two firs, picking up small pieces of garbage. Afterward, she and I sat on a log, stretching our legs out in the ferns. The low pulse of the Selway and Moose Creek converging in the distance seemed eternal. But pretty soon, we heard the buzz of Joe's plane coming to whisk us away.

"That girl was so sad," I said. "I hope Grandma wasn't like that."

My mother tossed her coffee dregs on the ground and wiped out her cup. "Most people can't survive this wilderness," she said. "But Mother did better here than in town." Her eyes got a hard look, as if she were seeing ghosts, seeing them but unafraid. Perhaps we were seeing the same thing.

Joe landed a few minutes later, and my mother launched into a story about the woman straight away.

"I saw her a couple days ago," said Joe, speaking slowly as if he had all the time in the world. "She asked for a ride out. Yeah, she was pretty upset. She was calling her boyfriend a son of a bitch."

"She was crying when she came to our camp," my mother said, worry wrinkled behind her frank eyes. "She was spent."

"Yeah," Joe said again. "She was a pretty bad case. I can't give free rides to everyone who walks in here and can't make it out or I'd go broke. You see a lot of people get back here and find they've taken on too much. But I told her I'd take her for free. She didn't want it."

He tapped his watch and said we needed to get going. Luckily, he added, it was not going to get over ninety degrees, and since there were just two of us and he had already transported most of the gear, we should be fine in the thinning air. In a matter of minutes, we were in our seats and buzzing up the airfield to lift off. The screaming engine took the small plane high over the confluence, over Freeman Peak, and above the folds of the mountain range. As I turned and watched Moose Creek Ranger Station fade from view, a sensation of tremendous loss overcame me.

In the years that followed, I would think of the woman almost as a phantom, appearing not exactly as a person but as a web of curious relationships between women and wilderness I was trying to unravel. The woman's hysterical crying, my mother's tears throughout our childhood, my grandmother's words to me before she died: "I didn't do right by your mother." Connie, vanished. And myself, always searching for something elusive.

At the time, though, I didn't consider any of this. The woman was a person in distress on whose behalf I had felt immense hope as she stood with my mother eating chocolate. When she left so abruptly, that feeling evaporated, and I was concerned for her safety, afraid of what might happen if she didn't get a ride out.

"Wow, what was that?" one of my brothers had said as the woman left our campsite.

"Shouldn't we do something?" I said.

"If she doesn't want to be rescued," my mother said, "there's nothing we can do." And I knew immediately that she was right, because this was wilderness, where people came to be left alone. Where people could disappear if they wanted to.

22 War

After my first visit to Moose Creek, I hiked or flew in every year for at least a few days, and sometimes Connie was there. One August, she and I were sitting on a rustic picnic bench at the station. "One year I spent three days riding around in a car with Nez Perce elders," Connie said, squinting

Standing woman; Mrs. Kanuakun-wak-wak on the Colville Reservation looking northeast, standing at the exact spot where Chief Joseph's teepee stood when he died, 1935. Lucullus Virgil McWhorter Photographs, Courtesy of Manuscripts, Archives, and Special Collections, Washington State University Libraries.

into the mellowing afternoon, "and we went to all these sites that were important to them, and they told me stories."

We'd just finished sorting through a pile of maps held in a wooden cabinet. Red wine in tin cups, sun behind us, airfield in front of us. I had my notebook, pen poised, ready to write. When Connie spoke, people took notes. They didn't let the stories slip away. She obviously felt the same about the elders. "I had a tape recorder going the whole time," she went on, "and the elders, they knew that. The recordings were for the Selway Assessment Project."

I asked if David Miles was in that car. He was the only Nimíipuu elder I'd actually met. After I had opened Esther's box, images of him flooded back to me. I recalled once, when I was in my twenties, I accompanied my grandmother to meet David at the Spokane airport. When he deplaned, he seemed to fill the terminal, seemed to dwarf the other travelers with his broad shoulders and strong arms. He was in a wheelchair. Esther ran up and hugged him with an enthusiasm I'd never witnessed, and a window opened for me into her world before I was born. She lifted her shoulder and pursed her lips like a schoolgirl. She and David had tickets to a Spokane minor-league baseball game, and they strolled off talking about the past as if I weren't there.

I remembered seeing David again a few years later on a ripe summer day much like that day at Moose Creek, vigorous as he talked about the Bible at Esther's request. David was an ordained minister, which impressed her. She lounged in a lawn chair under her walnut tree, I reclined on the grass, and we listened as he quoted Isaiah and explained the exodus of the Jews, and then the two lapsed into gossip about people they knew. David's voice, silky and commanding, and his hands, vibrantly expressing what the voice did not, is still clear to me.

I had known that David had grandchildren my age, and I vaguely wondered if they had spent time with my grandmother. I may have known that he and his family were from the same band as Hinmatóowyalahtqit, or Chief Joseph—I don't recall—but later I learned that the name he was given at birth, Two-Moons, came from the noted Nimíipuu warrior who had been at the Battle of the White Bird. That battle opened the Nez Perce War of 1877, which took them across the Bitterroots. But what struck me that day under the walnut tree was that I heard David and my grandmother talk about the Bitterroots, the only time I heard Esther mention the wilderness other than in her living room when I was sixteen. I don't recall specifics—they could have mentioned picking huckleberries, hunting at Old Man Lake, the Crags, Coolwater, 62 Ridge, could have discussed how his people's trails passed through Moose Creek or how her marriage began there—I only remember that the conversation gave Esther a lightness.

My grandmother would later write in her diary referring to that day: *David told lots of stories about early Indian life in Idaho. Only an Indian has experienced those things.* But I saw more in that memory, something that startled me. Through David's remembrances, my grandmother seemed to bloom like the bitterroot itself, the resurrection flower, small pink petals and fanning leaves with nourishing roots, the first plant to arrive in the spring. His knowledge must have put her in touch with times in her life when she was satisfied, reminded her of her affection for the land. I had the feeling of her leaning into the gift of a long friendship and into a past mood where she could be grateful for ordinary things like the shade of a walnut tree.

"David wasn't there," Connie said, snapping me back into the present. She lifted her cup as she gazed into the middle distance where generations of ponderosas stood along the airfield, sun in their needles, limbs raised as if they were singing. "It's Al Slickpoo I remember." Al Slickpoo knew everything about the Selway country, she said. He was the last person whose first language was Nez Perce.

"We drove to Pilot Knob," she said, conjuring a large rock with bulbous outcroppings. "We—white people—call it Pilot Knob, anyway, but Al called it Tam-loy-its-maxs, the spiritual mountain." She went on to explain that the Nimíipuu words for the land and its plants and animals were important. How else could you understand the wilderness if you didn't know the original names? "The Nez Perce pick berries and hunt there," she said. "It was a place where young people went for spiritual quests—and they still go there today, apparently. The elders were asking me, or, the Forest Service, really, to preserve Pilot Knob, even though we've already disturbed it by putting a fire lookout below the rock. Luckily, we haven't ruined the rock itself."

An airplane pilot with a scraggly beard and a clean-cut researcher from the University of Idaho who'd been helping Connie with the maps wandered out of the station to the picnic table and sat down, and I could feel Connie's story about the elders vanishing. Our conversation splintered into small talk, then lapsed into Forest Service politics—which rangers were better at protecting wilderness, who were sellouts. I sat silent, yawning, thinking we could have been in any old workplace where people jostle for position and power. Connie and the pilot exchanged stories about the Payette Forest, and the researcher turned to me and started mentioning places I'd never heard of. I nodded and kept yawning. Then we all slipped inside to eat and drink wine.

❦

There are events beyond a person's life that define their story. The words from the constellation guide at the retreat center probably stick stubbornly to the thorniest part of my grandparents' history because they help explain what I cannot. Before I had even met Connie, she sent me a book stamped with the insignia: *Moose Creek Ranger District Historical Information Inventory and Review.* She referred to it simply as the *Moose Creek History.* In that book I read about George beyond the little I'd gleaned from the family and Esther's *Memoirs,* beyond what Dick told me: "It's easy to see how life in the wilderness then, as well as now, constitutes an element of danger," the history states. "Perhaps it is easy to see why that type of life attracts only a few special kinds of people. Ranger George Case, who was one-quarter Cherokee, and his wife Esther were two such people."

That sentence—*Ranger George Case, who was one-quarter Cherokee*—sent me deeper into my search than I wanted to go, complicating the image I was drawing of this man, as if it wasn't complex enough. A more accurate statement would be that I was terrified of either possibility: that George was a Native American-wannabe, or that he had some verifiable relation to Native Americans that I would feel duty-bound to uncover. If George was an imposter, I would add it to the list of his flaws, more evidence of his roguery. But if he was legitimately linked to a Cherokee past, then his story would be more difficult for me, a person far removed from Indigenous experience, to interpret.

The Cherokee, of course, resided thousands of miles from the Selway-Bitterroot, which itself is the traditional homeland of the Nimíipuu. Still, I understood that the way the US government treated a tribe or band in the southeast part of the country was not unlike how they treated a tribe or band in the Midwest or Northwest. I saw, for example, a direct connection between the Battle of the Little Bighorn and the fate of the Nimíipuu. When Lieutenant Colonel George Armstrong Custer and two hundred of his men were killed by Lakota and Cheyenne warriors at the Little Bighorn, President Andrew Johnson immediately sent troops to Idaho to move the Nimíipuu onto a reservation. Johnson feared one man above all others: Chief Joseph, Nimíipuu leader and resister of American treaties. Joseph, Johnson thought, might organize another Little Bighorn, bigger, more threatening to westward expansion. I wondered how a maybe or maybe-not Cherokee man would have felt about these terrible events. They would have been recent history to George.

So I brought the *Moose Creek History* with me to lunch at a restaurant in Spokane and read the passage to my mom. *Ranger George Case, who was one-quarter Cherokee.* "Is it true?" I asked her. We were splitting a salad and French fries. She drank her soda, sucking her cheeks into the straw, and her angular face transformed into something soft and oblong.

"When we were kids, we used to go around telling people we were Indian," she said, passing the salad dressing. "I don't know where we got that idea. And Mom would say, *You hush up!* She didn't confirm or deny it."

"Did you ever ask her?"

She shrugged, furrowing her brow.

I asked why Esther never talked about George. "Was she ashamed of him? Was that why she was unhappy?"

"He tried to please her, but she wanted someone he wasn't. He did his best."

I didn't know what she meant. Sometimes she was vague like that. I surmised she might be referring to George's alcoholism, an addiction he developed after he left the wilderness, which I knew about because my Uncle Richard had written about it in no uncertain terms. Maybe I was striking too close to the bone, or my mother just wasn't interested. She stabbed the romaine and the cauliflower, swishing it in the dressing. She has always been much better than I am at living with uncertainty.

"Well, do you think George was part Native American?" I pressed her.

She threw me a casual smile and changed the subject, telling me about some precocious statement one of my nephews had made. Family trivia. Sigh.

The more she shifted away from the topic in the restaurant, the more I felt the pull of history in this shadowy grandfather. A history stretching beyond my mother and me, hitting on the sensitive topic of origins, where politicians and professors and celebrities and any number of people claim Native American ancestry, claim to be descended from the Cherokee, especially, who, with the Choctaw, Chickasaw, Creek, and Seminole, walked the Trail of Tears.

George, my mother offered, finally, had never claimed to be Cherokee as far as she knew.

"Then how did that story end up in a history book?" I asked.

She didn't know that either.

Perhaps someone along the line fabricated the ancestry to justify their use of recently seized Nimíipuu lands, of Indigenous displacement, I offered. "Or maybe it's just a typo," I said, hoping that by expressing lack of interest I might pry more information out of her.

"Maybe," she said. "There was a lot about him that nobody knew."

And with that, I knew I wasn't going to get an answer from my mother. George's ancestry didn't seem significant to her, so it shouldn't to me. Still, I remembered a long, winding road trip I took with Steph and my mother across the country and a stop at the Battle of the Little Bighorn, where she stood on the edge of the rough field, crying. Though I'd seen her cry plenty, I'd never witnessed a breakdown at a monument. Steph pulled my mother's sleeve and asked why she was sad, and she answered, "The white man didn't do right by the Indians."

❧

President Johnson's campaign against the Nimíipuu, the Nez Perce War, is known today as the Last Indian War, even though it was far from the last time the government would terrorize Indians. When Johnson sent the US Cavalry for Chief Joseph at the foothills of the Bitterroots, he and seven hundred men, women, and children drove two thousand horses over the mountains, believing they were leaving the war behind in Idaho.

But US militia were waiting in Montana on the other side, and they pursued the fleeing caravan for twelve hundred miles over four months. The Nimíipuu were camped forty miles from the Canadian border when the troops caught up, and after a long battle, Joseph surrendered in a now-famous speech: "My heart is sick and sad. From where the sun now stands, I will fight no more forever."

Some of the tribal coalition like Chief White Bird made it to Canada, but the remaining Nimíipuu were sent to Indian Territory with the Cherokee and other tribes, first to the Quapaw Agency in Oklahoma and then to Tonkawa, where they wallowed in sticky, swampy, confined areas. Joseph filed petitions to the government and even wrote to General O. O. Howard, who told him to quit complaining and "make a garden." Joseph persisted until the 268 Nimíipuu who had survived were allowed to return by train to Lapwai in Idaho, while Joseph was sent to Colville in Washington, where he died.

Like the Nimíipuu, scores of Native peoples asserted themselves against the reservation and allotment systems and kept their languages and traditions alive in residential schools. But no one knows how many others died of colonial diseases, starvation, and war from Columbus's first contact in the Bahamas in 1492 until the Nez Perce war of 1877, Joseph's war, the so-called Last Indian War, on the periphery of the Bitterroot Mountains.

↔

At Moose Creek Ranger Station that summer night with Connie, after dinner, after stories, long after the pilot and the researcher had gone to bed, I was stretched out on a cot on the porch, staring down the field. Connie came out and plopped down in the big rocking chair. I sat up, snuggled in my sleeping bag. The bats dipped and swerved in the moonlight. We could see the outline of Grizzly Saddle, Connie's spiritual place. She often said, "To breathe the air, to walk up the Moose Creek runway and look up the drainage and see this huge, big land, it does something for me every time."

"Do you have that tape you made with the elders?" I asked.

"I do, somewhere, but it's worthless. You know, when I got home and played it, it was all raspy and just awful. I was sick thinking about the stories. Just lost. Of course, they're not lost for the Nez Perce," Connie said. "But they are for me."

"When you're doing historical work," I said, trying to console her, "it's hard. Even when your recorder works, there are gaps. There's just no way to collect everything. There's no straight line through history." I may have been trying to console myself, too. Because I recalled that when David was in the hospital in 1994, on his deathbed, my mother brought Esther to see him. Esther called out David's name, but he didn't seem to recognize her. "It was very sad for Mother," my mother told me. By the time she related this information, my grandmother was gone, too, and I knew enough about the Bitterroots and what David's friendship meant to her to regret never having talked to her about it.

"Yeah," Connie said, "You try to put the pieces together."

"But sometimes the lost pieces are more evocative, and maybe they should just stay missing." I said this even though I knew immediately I would keep searching for those vanished pieces.

23 Diaries

Perhaps the single most important trip made by a white man through the Bitterroots was that of Gifford Pinchot. Pinchot, who had a wide smile and thick mustache, later became the first chief of the Forest Service in 1905 and founded the first forestry school in the United States, at Yale.

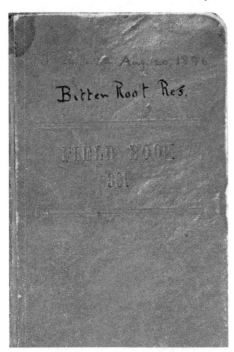

Gifford Pinchot's Bitterroot Reserve diary, 1896.
Courtesy of University of Idaho Library.

But before all that, in 1896, he surveyed what would become the Selway-Bitterroot Wilderness. It felt imperative to dig into Pinchot's story, especially when I learned that the famous conservationist John Muir was scheduled to accompany Pinchot on his Bitterroot trip, but at the last minute Muir couldn't go. The fact that Muir almost traveled to the Bitterroots was more seductive than if he'd actually walked the landscape, because if you almost do something and then back out, don't you leave behind a little envelope of desire?

And so, on July 27, Pinchot, without Muir but with two guides and a cook, traveled from Hamilton to Lost Horse Creek. It came as no surprise to me that Pinchot, like earlier travelers, kept a diary, where he complained about the perilous Bitterroot topography: *Trail worst I ever traveled as to rocks*, Pinchot wrote. The canyons were *extremely rocky and precipitous*. Mainly, though, he was interested in trees: old forest or new growth? Did they grow in stands or alone? Did they grow close to creeks or far away? How were they affected by fire? Sometimes he called trees *timber*, underscoring the fact that he was taking note of how profitable the land could be. He could be awestruck, too. When he came to one of the massive cedar forests that the Selway-Bitterroot is known for, he called it *magnificent*.

Though Pinchot was one of the first official foresters in America, he didn't understand how fire was essential to forest health, how the Nimíipuu knew about fire management long before white men did. Pinchot complained about how the flames had weakened the trees, and blamed Native Americans. *Practically no part of this region has escaped fire*, he wrote. *Very much of the prevailing thinness is due to fire, while the composition of the forest has been mainly determined by it. These fires are probably due in most cases to the Indians.*

It made perfect sense to me that Pinchot was obsessed with fire—that most divine element, symbol for enlightenment, knowledge, passion—when I learned that he was also given to mysticism. Throughout most of his adult life, he was in almost daily communication with his dead fiancée, Laura Houghteling. Pinchot and Laura had met and fallen in love at a popular high society resort in North Carolina. But Laura, a delicate, almost angelic woman (her nurse described her as "an angel of goodness"), had tuberculosis, which should have warned Pinchot away from becoming engaged. Somehow, though, he believed she would recover. When she died, he remained celibate, convinced he was married to Laura in a ghostly way. He wrote about her in his diary as if she were a living spirit. April 15, 1894: *A wonderful happy day, full of her presence and peace.* January 1, 1895: *Tonight my Dearest spoke to me, saying she wants to be with me as much as I want to be with her.*

In my search for the ghostly George, and haunted by Esther, I pored over Pinchot's early diaries, learning their code. When he wrote *A good day*, it meant Pinchot had communicated with Laura. *A beautiful happy day* was even better. *Not a clear day* meant that she hadn't been with him at all. I was even more fascinated by the fact that his *Bitterroot Reserve Diary* carried almost daily references to Laura along with notes on trees and fire. On the first three days of his trip, Pinchot reported: *A good day.* Things improved the next day: *A clear happy day.* The following day, communication faltered: *Not so clear a day*, and the next was worse: *Not a very good day*, as if her spirit was being absorbed by the forest. Then, she reemerged: *A better day.* This drama of Laura marked every footfall of Pinchot's Bitterroot trek, spiritual and physical worlds interfused. On his last day in the Bitterroots, he wrote: *A beautiful happy day*, and it was that day, when he felt close to her, that he gave the charge to preserve the Bitterroots— immediately. *They should be reserved without delay, and thereafter properly administered at the earliest possible moment*, he wrote, as if by protecting the land he was shielding his beloved.

Pinchot was no hero to the Nimíipuu. By the time he arrived in the Bitterroots, the land had been taken from them, and he was just another white man criticizing them for what we know today as sustainable forest practices. For this reason, it is a peculiar irony that the land would not have remained intact but for Pinchot's visit, would have been settled, developed, and monetized if Pinchot had not set it aside in 1896. In other words, if not for Laura, the Selway-Bitterroot country may never have been protected under the Forest Reserve Act, the National Forest System, and later, the Wilderness Preservation System. Today, the Nimíipuu have asked the US government to protect for their use a region of the wilderness known as láqsa, k'useyne'ískit, or the Trail to Buffalo Country, part of their original homeland. In the Nimíipuu's National Register of Historic Places application, they write: "Although there are some modern intrusions . . . the property's physical appearance and integrity of setting, feeling, and association remain intact in the eyes of the Nez Perce people who value and interact with the property on a regular and ongoing basis."

If not for Laura. How could I not see a direct line from Laura to Esther? Esther who, like Laura, protected the land without really knowing it. When George died in 1962, Esther showed up at his funeral with $25,000 cash in her purse. She'd sold George's wilderness land to a man—a swindler, my father called him—who then sold the land to the owners of Moose Creek Ranches, a conglomeration of old homesteads that fizzled out after a few years. The Forest Service bought Moose Creek Ranches in 1966 to make it part of the Selway-Bitterroot Wilderness.

↢

Today, Pinchot Creek is one of the widest, most spacious campsites along the Selway River. I've always wanted to stop at Pinchot to quietly celebrate Laura's ghost. One year I got the chance.

I journeyed into the wilderness with an archeologist I'll call Mark. He and his wife have helped preserve some of the most important Nimíipuu sites along the Selway River: longhouses and pit houses, village sites and campgrounds, stone tool scatters and cairns, and places for spiritual rituals and vision quests. I arranged to meet Mark—a fit man of sixty-five with slightly graying hair—at a Forest Service gravel road leading to the wilderness boundary in Idaho. We shrugged on our packs and I immediately quizzed him about the land—What were the Nimíipuu structures like? How many early homesteads had the Forest Service burned? Who had named Pinchot Creek, and did Pinchot really camp there? Mark was vague about details, saying the land and the tribe had secrets outsiders weren't supposed to know, and the Forest Service was equally protective of cultural resources. "Anywhere that's a good campsite for humans today was a good campsite for the Nez Perce and early homesteaders and foresters," was all he would say.

As we trudged up the trail, Mark mostly talked about his wife, who had died the previous year. "People say to me, *You need to get over it.* They tell me to move on. I'm never getting over it. I'm not moving on." He was insistent. Angry. His anger scared me a little. Though I knew this was grief, I didn't understand it, or perhaps I couldn't access it. I was disappointed in myself for not knowing how to comfort him. But I remember thinking, what I can do is listen, imagine his love for her, her love of plants, of travel, help him sort through the archeology of their marriage.

We made camp the first night halfway to Pinchot on the banks of the Selway. Dick had shown me photos of Nimíipuu arrowheads found along the river some fifty years earlier. I asked Mark about them. "Anywhere you see the bank cut away," he said, "there'll be artifacts." All I saw was a wide beach of fist-sized rocks in amber, tan, gray, and white. "Arrowheads, they'll have been flushed away. But the tools are too heavy. And the fire-scarred rocks." He plucked a rock the size of his palm from the shore and angled it my way: a human hand had chipped away pieces for arrowheads, creating a sharpened edge. The radiating grooves from the flaking resembled an alluvial fan, where multiple channels of a mountain river empty into a valley. "After they chipped off the arrowheads, they used the tool for pounding camas root," he said, carefully placing the rock in the exact spot where he'd found it. In the meantime, I had come across half of an insulator in the sand. The insulator was from the 1930s, when people like my grandfather had strung telephone lines between cabins and stations and lookouts. Now all of those wires had been removed, but a few artifacts remained.

I talked to Mark about my grandparents, my struggles to learn about them. I may have mentioned my mother and what I saw to be our dueling desires to possess familial memories. It's probable that we were both in confessional mode, because after dinner, Mark spoke about his wife so candidly that I was startled. Maybe the wilderness had released something in him, in us. In any event, he told me that she had kept diaries. He'd never read them throughout their married life—he respected her privacy—and besides, she kept them in a secret place. When she was dying, she asked him to get them for her, told him where to look. She could move a little—not much; it took most of her strength just to walk to the toilet. I felt as if I could see the diaries, six volumes of them, covered in flowered patterns to reflect her love of gardening and landscape. He set the books at her bedside. He didn't pay much attention to what she did with them after that. He gave her exquisite care, with the utmost attention, which took most of his energy. But he did remember her saying, "I wonder if anyone will read my diaries when I'm gone."

A few days later, she was gone.

After the funeral, after the guests and condolences, he was changing the bedding and there were her diaries sitting atop the linen in the closet in plain view. He thought she must have wanted him to read them. He sat down with a glass of wine one night by the fire and began. Page after page of memories, and some of those memories criticized him, the vacations he'd planned, camping trips, hikes into the wilderness. He couldn't really remember how many pages he read, but as the night waned, he felt terribly heavy.

We said good-night and retired to separate tents. The story burned through me. The grief I had been unable to feel on his behalf became real. As a longtime diary keeper, I understand the freedom and the essential constraints of the form. While diaries allow me to say whatever I want, they also bring me face-to-face with time's steady march, the inevitability of change, and ultimately of death. I thought of Esther's diary, how I drew solace from even her most troubling passages. In one of the last entries, she referred to a call from the Forest Service: *They want to give me a paid trip to Moose Creek on September 12. David called and said he would go with me. I have no desire to go back there. Fly or otherwise.* I had to accept this as her final word about a place I had learned to love but that represented such pain to her. At the same time, I drew comfort knowing that she had the friendship of David, a man whose people came from that land. I wondered, too, if Mark's wife's diaries were the strange, secret language of love, her giving him a reason to be angry at her dying, helping to emancipate him from the devastation of loss. It was a story of hiding and care, or maybe the two things at odds, like how digging up the past felt torturously contradictory, trying to find meaning in it and trying to let it go.

In the morning, after coffee, Mark and I turned back without making it to Pinchot. It was a clear day, and I felt surrounded by a lovely lucidity as we shuffled out of the forest together. But I would be hiding something myself if I didn't admit that to this day, I sometimes quake thinking about the delicate thread of story holding powerful women—Laura, Esther, and Mark's wife—together in the wilderness.

24 Mule

I don't know how long my grandmother stayed in bed in St. Maries when my mother was a teenager, but sometime in the 1950s, George sent her to the psych ward of a private hospital in Spokane. After a few months, she seemed to get better. Back at home, she ate full meals, slept regular hours, and attended the meetings of the Daughters of the American Revolution,

Mule corral at Moose Creek Ranger Station, 2005. DJ Lee photo.

which George and my mother interpreted as evidence of recuperation. Gradually, though, her interest in the DAR faded, and she crawled into bed again. Refused to eat. Grew bone thin. But she did read Christian Science literature and made marginal notes. I noticed she had underlined "To know death, or to believe in it, involves a temporary loss of God," in her Mary Baker Eddy volumes, and I knew I was glimpsing the dark silver glow of despair that comes before a full fall into depression.

By the time my mother revealed these things about my grandmother's illness, it had been several years since my summer of volunteering at Moose Creek. But what she told me put me in mind of the mules I'd handled at the station, especially the day Gabe said, "If you want to learn about wilderness…" and dropped a pile of *Western Mule* magazines in front of me.

"A whole magazine devoted to mules?" I said.

He didn't seem amused. "The backcountry was made *by* mules, *for* mules." He was moving around the kitchen cooking breakfast.

"Not exactly *Vogue* models," I said. Each issue featured a mule on its cover. A red-shirted cowboy with a beer gut riding a mule, a young woman in full rodeo regalia stroking a mule's neck, a plump couple on two mules against autumn foliage.

"There's a myth about mules being stubborn, but what they've really got is a strong sense of self-preservation, a strong sense of history." I was curious. Another animal, besides the human animal, with a strong sense of history? "A mule, once something bad happens, it's always bad," he went on. "If a mule gets stuck in a bog, she'll remember that for the rest of her life and you might never get her over a boggy trail again. A horse? You could coax her over that bog a million times." I'll never forget what he said next: "Mules carry mental baggage."

Mental baggage. When my grandmother went to bed a second time, George didn't know what to do, how to help. Esther knew of a Christian Science hospital in Puyallup, hundreds of miles from St. Maries. The hospital was expensive, but the language of Christian Science spoke to her as nothing else did. "Dad had squirreled away his Forest Service pension checks and he pooled that money with my teenage savings," my mother said. The notations in Esther's Mary Baker Eddy volumes from that time indicate a desire to separate mind from body, to become pure spirit, and part of me could see the draw of that, especially if she was on the brink of depression.

"I remember taking the train to Puyallup by myself," my mother told me. She was fifteen. She described the dingy white halls, old women with cruel eyes and dry voices cackling, "Hello dearie." Heavy double doors opened, a nurse came through, and there sat Esther in a wheelchair. My mother didn't recall what they talked about, just the doors opening again and the nurses wheeling her mother away.

If I had to guess, I'd say my grandmother's mulishness, her inability to let go of the past, was part of what attracted George in the first place. He had a special affinity for mules, an aspect of him I didn't understand until I spent that summer at Moose Creek and learned that almost everyone who hangs out with the creatures ends up loving them. The way they interact with people—they are as playful and coy and personable as they are stubborn—is charming. George's films flicker with mule teams weighed down with panniers while they wind over mountain passes or cross streams. In one of my favorite sequences, in what is clearly Moose Creek Ranger Station, he has strung together a three-mule team and placed a small child of no more than three years old—my Uncle Richard—on the lead horse. Running along the bottom of the film clip is the caption, "Dick learns to pack."

Western Mule chronicled how the curious animals were the spine of American progress, seemed to say that it wasn't railroads, immigrants, slavery, Native American genocide, the industrial revolution, barbed wire, war, or architecture that made America. These sweeping tragedies and technologies played a part, but under it all, mule power created America, especially the West. Needless to say, the idea toppled my own sense of history, and I said so to Gabe.

"You think any other animal could walk these mountains with so much on its back?" he quipped. He had a point. I had often stopped to watch the creatures cock their ears, snort, squeal, and swat flies with their tails. They seemed powerful, impossibly strong. They intimidated me. I was so convinced I couldn't handle the animals that I wouldn't walk within ten feet of the fence. Yet I was inexplicably attracted to the mules, to Tank, in particular, taller than the rest with large hooves and a sleek black coat. Whenever I sauntered by, always at a distance, Tank made a high-pitched laughing sound, whinnied, raised his tail, and pawed the ground as if he were ready to run away with me.

A few days later, Gabe said, "I need you today." The fences around the pasture bothered Gabe. "Inefficient," he called them. Nails were falling out and rails broken. The elk had cracked them to feed on the rich grasses that were reserved for horses. The fence would never be strong because the Wilderness Act outlawed power tools, Gabe said. "It's worth it, though. You start allowing power tools and it's all over."

After breakfast, we got to work digging new postholes. Though I didn't fully understand then the logic behind wilderness advocates' no-power-tools rule juxtaposed with an airfield carved down the middle of the compound, I could feel Gabe's conviction in every slash of the shovel against the soil. Hours passed. The temperature climbed into the nineties. Every time I heard the drone of an airplane, I felt the urge to run back to the station and mark it down in the spiral notebook. "I don't want to lose count," I said.

Gabe told me not to worry. "You think the Forest Service does anything with the statistics we keep back here? What're bureaucrats in DC gonna do with a list of how many planes landed in a wilderness one summer?"

I held a cross beam between two posts as Gabe pounded, one after another. Dig, plant post, refill hole, and nail, and six hours later he stretched his back, removed his ball cap, and wiped his brow with a handkerchief. "I'm packing out early tomorrow," he said, taking a long drink from his water bottle. He wiggled the fence. It barely budged. "This is strong enough to keep out the elk."

That night, exhausted, I lit the propane lanterns in the dwelling. Cool night air and the seesaw rhythm of the crickets filtered through the screen door. I sank into the rocking chair and closed my eyes for a few minutes. A loud crash startled me. I flung open the door to a ceiling of stars and a waxing crescent moon. Dark shapes were moving on the airfield. My eyes adjusted. Mules. Every evening when the planes stopped landing, Gabe released the mule team onto the airstrip to graze, and at dawn he ushered them in the corral. I was admiring their forms when the crash sounded again and I realized, with sudden horror, what was happening. I slipped into my shoes, grabbed a headlamp, and ran down the field a quarter mile, stumbling at the hooves of Tank, who was ready to spring forward into the fence that Gabe and I had spent the day mending. Several other mules were gathered behind Tank like a cheering section. Scrambling to my feet, I screamed, "Tank, NO." He swished his tail and froze. Maybe I did have authority over these giants. But when I turned to walk back up the airfield, I heard another splinter. Tank and I locked eyes for a moment. He turned his head, ears cocked back in annoyance and slammed into the fence again.

It was past midnight. Gabe had to rise at 3:30 a.m. to ride out, and I couldn't bear to wake him. Tank snorted. "Tank!" I yelled. "You're humiliating me. Please, just quit!" Tank flipped his ears, but he stopped. I cruised back up to the dwelling, and as soon as the screen door shut, I heard Tank at it again. What choice did I have? I dragged myself up the hill to the packer's cabin, stood on the porch. "Gabe," I said in a sturdy voice. "You asleep?"

No answer.

"*Gaaaabe?*" I knocked softly. "Tank's killing the fence."

Gabe emerged in blue boxers, cowboy boots, and no socks or shirt, his mop of dark hair flying. He strode past me and jogged down the field. I followed. "Hey!" he said. "Knock it off!" He ran circles around the mules, whistling and waving his arms until he'd herded the whole team down the field away from the fence. On his way back to the packers' cabin, he passed me without a word. I shouldn't have felt so terrible at not being able to control a mule team, but I did.

Early the next morning, coffee in hand, I met Gabe at the barn where he'd hitched his horse Hercules to the fence and was tying boxes to the Decker pack saddles strapped to the mules. "Hey, I need you to babysit the mules today." He said he had to pick up some garbage at Elbow Bend. "Connie found a cache with a bunch of shit in it. I'm taking five head, and Hercules. I'm leaving Dexter, Izzy, Earl, and Tank with you."

Tank's ears perked up. "Yeah, Tank definitely respects my authority," I said. "Really, Gabe. How do you babysit a mule?"

"They'll get restless without Hercules." Mules, he explained, because of their confused identity—a cross between a donkey and a horse—were usually calm with their female horse around, but they would get nervous later in the day without her.

"I can't," I said. "I'm afraid of Tank."

"You'll be fine." He said *fine* by drawing the word out, as if I were ridiculous.

Gabe worked intently, whispering to Flo as he packed her. "You're beautiful," he said. "You could be a movie star." Gabe told me I could touch her, and when I cautiously ran my hand over the taut roundness of her rear and she didn't move, I felt a strange power, which I linked to her sweet, grassy scent. He pointed to an aluminum bucket filled with balls of sawdust. "It's their cake." I noticed the balls were not sawdust but actually discs of oats. His instructions were simple. I would let them out on the field at dusk. In the morning I would hit the aluminum bucket with a trowel. "The mules will know. It means they're getting their cake. They'll come running into the corral and you shut the gate."

"So they don't get the cake except tomorrow morning?"

"That's right. Oh, they'll try to get you to—. They'll start braying and screaming, but you can't give in."

If they start screaming, ignore them. Okay. I could do that, except I must have looked concerned, because Gabe added, "You gotta be like a mule. Don't give in."

We walked the corral as I said their names: Dexter had a line down his back; Earl, a white nose; Izzy was black. And Tank. Well, I knew Tank: tall, dark, and handsome.

Gabe climbed onto Hercules and headed off with his team.

⌁

I'm not sure what I did with my morning, but I probably daydreamed about my grandmother, because I spent that summer trying to figure out why she'd lost her mind for a while. I saw her huddled at the bed's edge, wadding the quilt into a ball tucked under her chin, staring beyond the bedroom into the void. According to my mother, Esther came home from the Christian Science hospital, and again, she seemed better for a while, but then she fell into an even deeper pit. For George there was no choice. "He didn't know what else to do," my mother told me. "He'd exhausted all the options." That's when he asked Esther to go to Orofino.

Orofino is an hour's drive from the ridge where Esther was raised, another hour from the wilderness trailheads I've used many times to access the Bitterroot Mountains. During Esther's lifetime, Orofino was home to Idaho's second mental asylum, dubbed the Idaho State Sanitarium, known today as State Hospital North. I don't know what kind of rumors she'd heard about the place, but I'm certain she must have known something. In my research, I learned that in 1905 the sanitarium was built to house an ever-expanding population of troubled souls in Idaho, where people could be tried for insanity and the guilty committed against their will.

Esther must have refused Orofino, because my mother found herself at the St. Maries courthouse presenting evidence of her own mother's mental deterioration. "It was awful," my mother said about standing in front of the town judge. "But my heart went out to the judge, too, sitting in his wheelchair with his pomaded hair. He was unable to use his legs and hands since he'd crushed his spine in a logging accident. They'd made him judge because he couldn't log anymore." My mother didn't remember what she and George told that judge, but whatever it was, he committed Esther. I can only imagine how terrible that must have been for someone who held Baker Eddy's belief that "a physical diagnosis of disease—since mortal mind must be the cause of disease—tends to induce disease." The self-blame, the shame, the idea that she brought her illness on herself had to have made her worse. But part of me accepts that George didn't know what else to do in the face of Esther's declining health.

It was the one-hundred-mile car trip my mother remembered most, because irony, lightness, in the face of whatever the world throws her way is part of how she copes. The little family of three drove over a mountain pass and headed down the Clearwater River, road lined with granite bluffs. When they got to the sanitarium, George opened the door. I envision him offering his hand to help Esther out of the car and seeing she was missing a shoe. "Mother had thrown her shoe out the window somewhere along the way," my mother explained. "Once we figured out what happened, I told Dad we'd better go back and get it. I said, *Mom can't go into that place with one shoe.*"

And that's what they did.

That lone shoe in the ditch, a thing without its pair and therefore of no use, a parallel to her own situation, lodged in my imagination, an image I have returned to. The shoe was my grandmother's way of resisting, putting her foot down, stopping the moment. My mother's giving my grandmother the dignity of that shoe was the most tender act of love I could imagine.

Torture chamber. When I visited Esther at the Care Center right before she died, I hadn't associated the nursing home with the state hospital, the last time she'd been institutionalized. But since then, I've crawled inside her asylum days again and again, the white enamel walls, puffy-faced nurses, mechanical beds, blue electrical currents, and the numbness afterward, the sense of violation, the thought of having to submit repeatedly to electric shock treatments, more than twenty of them. Esther detested electric shock as much as her namesake Esther Greenwood in Sylvia Plath's *The Bell Jar.* When I imagine my grandmother, she's sitting in an alcove covered with a white gauzy blanket dreading her next round. One of the many tortures of electric shock is memory loss, but Esther emerged from those shocks with a sharp recollection of the past and a stubborn resolve not to talk about it.

It's impossible to say what made Esther turn the corner: hospitalization or George's death. Either way, the two events that made my grandmother well, I believe, formed a wall between Esther and my mother, and between my mother and me. My mother had no choice but to meet Esther's absence from the family home, her forays into hospitals, and George's sudden death with a steely resolve, the same resolve she saw in Esther and then passed on to me. As a therapist once told me, such resolve can see a person through the toughest of times, but often at the cost of vulnerability, the true passageway to intimacy.

Several years after my grandmother was gone, I visited Orofino. State Hospital North sits outside of town up a long, paved driveway lined with pines and firs, like a park. I needed to see the place where Esther had felt so tortured. The buildings, white stucco or brick, sedate and proper, are protected by high cyclone fencing. The building where Esther stayed is now a women's prison, which struck me as a cruel irony, but then the borders between asylums and prisons have always been fluid. Bales of barbed wire wind along the top and a central surveillance tower sits in the center.

I drove a service road above the prison and stepped out to take a breath and meditate on the building. I pulled out my camera and started snapping, and within minutes, a police car flashed behind me and out stepped an officer, her bust smashed into a bulletproof jacket. She held up her badge—Officer Westby—and told me to leave. "It's illegal to photograph a state prison," she said. I told her about my grandmother. She nodded sympathetically and said, "You still need to leave."

⦵

"Mules don't forget," Gabe had said, "and that makes them smart, surefooted." I had always seen my grandmother as the most foot-sure, capable, sturdy person in my life. It was a revelation to know that those qualities came from her "mental baggage." Maybe that's why she was cautiously drawn to the animals. One clip of George's films shows her leading mules with small children on their backs through a pasture. But more radically, a passage in her *Memoirs* details how she and George put their infant daughter Barbara in a ration box on one side of a mule balanced on the other side with a load of lumber as they rode the steep trails along the Selway River, how they trusted the mule as much as they trusted themselves.

Early evening on the day I was babysitting Gabe's mules, I was on the airfield pulling pine saplings, nervously waiting for the animals to begin crying for their horse, for their cake, for who knows what else, and when they finally did, a sort of horse whinny that morphed into a donkey bray, I was relieved. I glanced toward the corral. Swishing, stomping. I started hiking back to the dwelling as their screaming grew louder and steadier. On the way, I noticed the cracked fence rails from Tank's shenanigans the night before. In the barn, I found a hammer, shovel, and a few stray nails in the dirt of the floor. Just then, an otherworldly sound rang through the compound. Mournful and utterly primeval. I stepped out and Tank's head was hung over the corral fence, eyes glimmering. He screamed again. Though Gabe had told me Tank broke fences because he thought the grass was always greener on the other side, I wondered if there was something more to it.

"What happened to you?" I said. "What makes you destroy fences? Scream?" He angled his ears back as if he were going to snap at me, and then he went soft. I felt compelled to touch him. I placed my hand on his massive neck, then rubbed it until his muscles relaxed a little. He kept his head on the fence but he looked peaceful. Another mule whined. I made my rounds, stroking, talking quietly, overwhelmed by their colossal strength and the ancient knowledge in their dark eyes.

25 Low Knob

October 25, 2018

I want to blame.

I stare out the window at the neat little houses in my Moscow neighborhood, too neat in the gray morning. I want to blame the hunters. I want to hold a bear or cougar or wolf responsible, call to account a falling tree, an unmaintained trail, a criminal, the weather. But I know I'm throwing culpability outward because deep-down, I wonder if I am to blame.

Almost every time I talked with Connie, I asked her about people who had vanished in the wilderness. It was my way of wondering what happened to my grandparents, but it must have felt to her as though I had a morbid obsession with mountain tragedies.

One time when I was visiting her home in Nezperce, she told me about an older woman she'd met in the Selway-Bitterroot who embarked on a day hike one July. The woman and her five companions had planned to reach a place called Low Knob and loop back to their vehicle. The trip would take a few hours, and thus they didn't pack food or maps and wore only shorts and tank tops. Somehow they missed the loop and zigzagged down the wrong side of the knob, rambling aimlessly through pines and firs and knotted roots for a few hours. Then a cold rain settled in. "It wasn't extraordinary for weather," I recall Connie saying, "but you have to be prepared, even for a little shower, in these mountains." Toward evening, the older woman started shivering uncontrollably. I remember Connie's steady tone, all the wisdom and stoicism that lived in her throat, as she said, "They left her by a tree and split up to find a way out. They thrashed around all night until they found their route and, in the morning, they began walking her out." While Connie trained her marble-blue eyes on the mountains in the distance, which we could see from the big picture window of her house, I felt the shade of the story closing in, even before she said it: "Within fifteen minutes of arriving at their vehicle, the woman collapsed and died."

Maybe I was drawn to such stories not because they were tragic, but because lost things feel vivid and meaningful in a way the not-lost do not. Loss puts us in our place in the same way wilderness does, confronts us with lack of order and control and the fleeting nature of existence.

⌁

That afternoon, new hope comes through the newswire when, miraculously, Ace arrives at Moose Creek: "Ace, the border collie who belongs to Connie Johnson, was discovered about fifteen miles from the hunting camp where Johnson was last seen in the Fog Mountain area near Big Rock in the Selway River district. Idaho County Sheriff Doug Giddings confirmed early today that Ace showed up at a camp where private searchers who had been hired by the Johnson family were located. 'They didn't find the dog; the dog found them,' Giddings said. 'There's a possibility that if we would take the dog back in there, he might lead us to where she was,' the sheriff said. 'But that's the only possibility there is. We've searched everywhere; we believe she's in there, we just don't know where. It's possible the dog might go back to where she is.'"

It's possible. What I really want to know is how Connie and Ace spent those days and hours together. What she told him, how he snugged into her, kept her warm, how they shivered together against the weather, how he kept silent when the moose and bear sauntered by, how he crept out of their home, how he smelled his way back to Moose Creek.

Ace. Border collie, guardian. One soul knows what happened, and this makes Connie a little less lost.

26 Halftones

Almost a decade after Esther died, I made a four-hour drive to Travelers' Rest State Park in Lolo, Montana, on the edge of the Selway-Bitterroot. The park is hidden in the landscape. A long gravel driveway surrounded by bromegrass fields leads to the interpretive center, bookstore, and park offices. It was a late autumn day, and the cottonwood, aspen, and birch burned in gemstone tones. When I got out of the car, I heard Lolo Creek rattling in the distance.

I was greeted by Vernon, a man in a black leather jacket and with a long gray ponytail, who ran the place. He mentioned he was a Blackfeet Indian as he showed me around the display cases containing samples of the Lewis and Clark Expedition journals and tools the group had used. Since I was the only visitor, we went into Vernon's office—a metal desk, messy bookshelf, and one high window—to talk.

Travelers' Rest is the most important campsite of the Lewis and Clark Expedition, which took place from 1804 to 1806. The two captains were accompanied by thirty or so white men, the African American explorer York, and later the Shoshone Indian Sacagawea, her son with Toussaint Charbonneau, and the Shoshone guide Pike Queenah or Swooping Eagle. Although the expedition is a tired and contentious story in US history, I became fascinated with it when I learned that the Bitterroots nearly did them in. Some of their horses fell down ravines, they found little food, and at one point they had to tie rags to their naked, wounded feet to go on. The expedition officers were not given to complaints, except when crossing the Montana and Idaho mountains. They called the Bitterroots a "stoney bad land," and a "horrible mountainous desert." The expedition would not have survived without the help of Nimíipuu guides.

Tzi-Kal-Tza [or Daytime Smoke] around 1865. Courtesy of Wisconsin Historical Society.

Lewis wrote on June 27, 1806: "We were entirely surrounded by those mountains from which to one unacquainted with them it would have seemed impossible ever to have escaped; in short without the assistance of our guides I doubt much whether we who had once passed them could find our way to Travellers rest."

The first question I asked Vernon was about the expedition's effects on the Nimíipuu. Thomas Jefferson ordered the expedition to gather information about the tribes they met as they traveled, not just the Nimíipuu, but the Osage, Lakota, Cheyenne, Crow, Mandan, Blackfeet, Salish, Shoshone, Spokane, Yakima, and others, and Lewis, especially, followed those orders, keeping meticulous accounts complete with drawings. Vernon leaned back into his chair and spoke in a calm, steady voice about how Lewis came West believing that America was destined to run from coast to coast. What was really disturbing about Lewis was that he attempted to categorize the Indians he met without fully understanding how intricate Native social and political structures were. If you read Lewis's journals all the way through, Vernon said, you could see him following the linear, European model of classifying people in order to control them.

"Lewis really began the thought process of not appreciating the complexity of Native people that went right through to the establishment of reservations," Vernon continued as he raised his expressive gray eyebrows and looked over his glasses, not smiling, but not scowling either. "That's one of the most significant things about his life and death. He was the beginning of the opening of the West. Lewis made the template for how this country was going to deal with Native peoples, and it has always struck me how little he understood. Whenever you try to establish some kind of order, but you don't really have the skill or understanding, you're going to mess it up."

Looking back, I'm fairly certain Vernon was not implying that I was messing things up with my questions, but I sometimes wonder if that was exactly what I was doing. A few months after my meeting with him at Travelers' Rest, I would fly across the country to Cherokee County on a naïve quest to establish some kind of order to my family tree. Cherokee County is shouldered into the border of Oklahoma and Missouri in the extreme southeast corner of Kansas. Columbus, a town of three thousand, is the county seat and George's hometown.

I remember how nervous I was as I parked at the end of Main Street and shuffled up the sidewalk. Nervous, but full of anticipation, wondering how much had changed since George was a boy. Quiet streets, clapboard houses, storefronts. One coffee shop, one or two diners. A concrete-and-marble World War I memorial towering over the town square, the names of young men, George's dead classmates, chiseled into the granite. When I saw that memorial, I envisioned my grandfather, twenty years old and having just escaped a hell that killed sixteen million and wounded twenty million more, seeing the monument staring him in the face in the center of his own home.

I checked into a hotel. The clerk directed me to the Cherokee County Genealogical-Historical Society. Inside the modest building, three eager women greeted me: Elsa—wide face, thick glasses and limbs, in a floral smock shirt; Agnes—dark hair, eyes, and skin, in jeans; and tall, stately Mary, who in her younger days might have dressed in Scarlett O'Hara attire, complete with crinoline and ruffles.

"Anything we can do!" they said, almost in unison. They became my good fairies.

Elsa opened spools of microfilm, boxes of old newspapers, files of photographs, and some of the rolls and registers of the Cherokee Nation. In three days sifting through census records and obituaries, I learned that George's father had grown up in Indiana and his mother in Oklahoma. I tracked down his mother's family name: Childers.

"Childers is a Cherokee and Creek name," Elsa said.

"Sometimes," Agnes corrected her. "Sometimes not."

The three of us scoured the register and census shelves and located a number of Childerses, one with George's mother's name Alice, but the date of birth didn't match.

"If your grandfather was in high school here, we do have old year-books," Agnes said.

Yearbooks. A source I'd never considered in all my years of searching. The women disappeared into a back room and emerged with the *Checoukan*, the Cherokee County High School yearbooks from 1910 to 1920. The shaggy, rugged George of the Moose Creek photos resembled the images in the *Checoukan*—same sharp face and squinting eyes—but in the yearbook, George was clean cut. The images didn't surprise me as much as what I learned about him as a young man. He was an honors student who belonged to the forensic debating club, the YMCA, and the engineer-ing society, but his main activity was journalism—writing, storytelling. George ran the school newspaper and wrote columns for the town paper, his byline popping up again and again in short, humorous features and articles on politics and warfare, what seemed to me as I sat in the historical society to be rivers of ink and mountains of stories. He even wrote a satire in the tradition of Jonathan Swift's "A Modest Proposal" criticizing the "preparedness movement," mocking fearmongers and advocates of US military aggression.

I'd witnessed George's love of narrative in the 16 mm films. Still, all this time I'd thought my grandmother and her father, the downcast Edward, were my literary ancestors. I never thought to consider George, because no one spoke of him, and apparently he didn't speak for himself. Suddenly, sitting among the open yearbooks, I understood my grandfather differently. And I viewed Esther's silence as stubbornly excluding him from the family. I wanted to be angry. Except, the box. She must have known where it would lead me.

The truth is, even after lunch with my mother, when she told me she had no idea where the myths of George's Cherokee ancestry originated, I continued to piece things together because the story kept presenting itself to me in oddly insistent ways. One summer while at Moose Creek, Connie retrieved for me an oral history transcript by a man named Turner, where I read tales of bounty hunting cougars and chasing poachers through the woods. I came upon the passage: "George Case was the ranger at Moose Creek when I went in there. I remember him quite well. He was one-quarter breed Indian from Oklahoma country—Cherokee. Will Rogers was Cherokee, too." I cringed. Indian as entertainer, as celebrity.

I didn't know what to do with that information, so I tucked it away in a file. Then, a year or two later, Dick introduced me to a Moose Creek old-timer named Punk Wolfinbarger. Punk lived in a single-wide trailer outside Victor, Montana, a speed bump along Highway 93. When Dick and I arrived, Punk, a small, bald man with a flirty grin even at eighty-nine, was relaxing in an easy chair, sipping on a Hottie, a Montana craft beer with flames running up the can. To me, Punk gave the impression of a slow-moving stream you could sit by for hours.

Immediately, Dick buzzed over to Punk and pushed a photo toward his face. "Now that's up at the Origin Point, and those are Chinook salmon," Dick said, pulling out other photos, and the two reminisced. Having grown up with brothers, I was used to listening to men talk until their talk ran out. Then I opened my computer, where I'd downloaded George's movies, knelt beside Punk's easy chair, and rolled the films.

Punk squinted. "Why that's Moose Creek," he said, an unmistakable strain of joy in his voice.

I told him George was my grandfather, that he'd made the movies.

"I worked for George!" Punk said.

I wasn't exactly knocked off my feet, since Dick had taken me to visit the old-timer precisely because he'd known George. But I admit I was filled with a slow, satisfying, long-lasting kind of awe, to be speaking with the last person on Earth who'd known George in the wilderness.

I asked Punk what he remembered.

A television was playing in the corner. Punk's eyes jumped with the screen for some minutes. I waited, tempering expectations, reminding myself Punk was almost ninety and drinking a Hottie at one in the afternoon.

"You know what I remember about George?" he said, finally. "That old bugger'd be talking to you, and he'd just turn around a little and take a pee. He just turned and peed, and he'd keep talking. That's a fact. Right in the middle of the conversation. That's the way he done 'er." Punk took a swig. "George was Indian." Blurted it out, just like that, went straight from George's social pissing to Indian.

"Was he?" I said. I told him I'd heard rumors and asked if George told people he was Indian, or where that story came from.

I remember Punk licked the lid of his beer can and said, "I really wouldn't know," and rocked his chair a few times as if to close the conversation down. Dick and I left shortly afterward.

⌖

Of the many unsettling aspects of the Lewis and Clark Expedition, I was most bothered by their repeated references to their "friendly relations" with Native women. I learned that they even carried mercury pills to prevent venereal disease. They never let on if they fathered children, but they probably did, and certainly some of the Nimíipuu tribal members claim the story of Tzi-Kal-Tza, Halahtookit, or Daytime Smoke, son of a supposed union between Clark and a Nimíipuu woman. Daytime Smoke's photos are splashed across the Internet; he's a small man with long, dark hair. His story emerges in histories like Alan V. Pinkham and Steven R. Evans's *Lewis and Clark Among the Nez Perce*, and in a display in the Nez Perce National Historical Park near Lewiston. Easily findable online is a man claiming to be a Colville with the surname Clark, who surmises he and his siblings descended from the famous explorer.

As with my ancestral history, the more troubled I was by the story of Daytime Smoke, the less able I was to verify its truth. Sometimes I believed Daytime Smoke's mixed identity was mostly accurate, sometimes highly likely, sometimes pure fiction. It wasn't until I understood that what mattered less than the truth of the story was the fact that it was told at all, as if the expedition's trek through the Bitterroots and their rescue by the Nimíipuu needed a flesh-and-blood offspring, that I could embrace it fully.

Embracing the story meant accepting the paradox of Daytime Smoke and to a lesser extent, of George. Because whoever Daytime Smoke was, it seems certain that he fled in 1877 with Joseph and the other nontreaty Nimíipuu over the Bitterroots while they were being chased by the US Army. It was not at all extraordinary for Daytime Smoke to join with the only family he'd ever known, but his journey was a stinging irony: Daytime Smoke, made from Lewis and Clark's opening of the West, was also made to fight against the terror of that opening. The further irony for me was that Daytime Smoke, like Joseph and the other fleeing Nimíipuu, was deported to Quapaw, Oklahoma, a few miles from Cherokee County and George's hometown.

I will always remember how on my last afternoon at the Cherokee County Genealogical-Historical Society, the three women tidied up, pushing in chairs and straightening books. I didn't have much time, but in the final five minutes at the microfilm machine poring over the half-tones of old newsprint, it occurred to me that if George wrote for the newspaper, he also read it and would have seen the dozens of articles extolling the virtues of the American West. A full-page spread in 1915 enticed people to vacation at the great backbone of the continent, already designated the Rocky Mountain National Park, where visitors could find "more than forty species of plant" and "many kinds of wild life." Seven years later, George would go farther, to the Selway-Bitterroot, building a cabin in the presence of elk and moose and martens, dreaming of an

Idaho woman who might join him. As I packed up my things and walked out, I knew I would never unravel the threads of his ancestry or how he felt about it, whether he saw himself as a bridge between cultures, ways of life, or a bridge that was simply impassable.

Equally, I'll never forget how at Travelers' Rest, after Vernon and I talked for several hours, he asked if I wanted to walk the fifty-five-acre property, which was, he said, the only site along the entire Lewis and Clark trail where the Park Service had forked out money for aerial infrared photography and first-rate archeologists. They'd found artifacts—a button, a piece of metal, and the remains of latrines—proving the expedition had camped there. In their investigations, Vernon explained as we strolled the park, they also found Native American fire pits, flint tools, and arrowheads, establishing Travelers' Rest as a significant campsite for all kinds of tribes and bands who had moved through the area from time immemorial. A meeting place of cultures, histories.

A bridge led across Lolo Creek, and we stopped there, leaning on the railing and listening to water fall over boulders. It had rained earlier that morning and a lovely fresh scent permeated the air.

27 Marten

Pine martens are shy creatures rarely seen in the wild. There's a macabre reason for this. On the early frontier, because martens were highly prized for their glossy sable fur, they became one of the most hunted, persecuted animals in the American West. I confess, with some embarrassment, that the one time I saw this reclusive creature in the wild, I didn't even know what it was.

In over a decade of hiking the Selway-Bitterroot, I have backpacked to George's former homestead property at a place called Three Forks with my father and my mother and other family members, with Myron and Steph, and with friends. George's original cabin footings are wedged into the earth at Three Forks, rimmed by hawthorn and cedar. And then, some twelve years after my grandmother died, I made an effort to camp at Three Forks alone. Alone but with ghostly company. I had with me an oral history

Mrs. Charlie Johnson. Selway-Bitterroot Wilderness. No date. Courtesy of Dick Walker Historic Photo Collection.

transcript and an MP3 recording Dick had given me. The history was spoken by Fae Smith, George's closest neighbor, about the time when the two were bachelors living in the wild in the 1920s.

I assembled my camp chair, put on my headphones, and Fae's high-pitched voice sang in my ears. "There was more cabins in here at Three Forks when the trappers and prospectors was here than when we came in homesteading." On previous visits, I'd imagined George in his sixteen-by-sixteen-foot log cabin waking with the dawn, fetching water, chopping wood, always alone. But Fae was describing a bustling community. From Fae I learned that George spent his time there hunting, growing vegetables, picking fruit, and making photographs and movies with giant black cameras. What else did he do?

"Ol' George used to strip off stark naked, you know. He'd strip off out there and be hoeing corn there naked for hours. One time I yelled out to George, People's a coming! And George ran and got his clothes on. But no one was coming!" Fae laughed into my ear and I heard the playfulness of the prank. Still, George hoeing without clothes. It was a story I'd encountered in multiple sources, a stunt he was known for. It sounded edgy, like the account of him peeing while talking to a group of people, resisting basic norms, especially in a corner of the Bitterroots crammed with trappers, prospectors, homesteaders, and Nimíipuu families. But with the sun on my back and the sky an azure blue, I could see how this place might make a person want to strip down and wrap themselves in a garment of summer light.

A few feet away from where I had set up my tent lay a sizeable mound of rocks, deliberately placed, like some kind of ancient grave marker. I'd seen the rock pile on previous visits, had speculated with family and friends on what it could be. A root cellar? An altar? A monument? A tomb? It was a relief to hear Fae's oral history explain it. Fae and George stored ammunition in the shed attached to George's cabin. Besides that, George had a can of ether he'd stolen from the Medical Corps during World War I. Fae and George were hunting one day when they heard a series of blasts and then a deafening explosion. They ran back a quarter of a mile in time to see the roof blown off George's cabin, the log structure—George's home—engulfed in flames, and the chimney collapsing into a pile of rocks.

According to Fae, George treaded into the burning cabin and emerged coughing and carrying packsaddles, blankets, and Fae's Dutch oven. It wasn't just the details of the explosion, but Fae's quaint vernacular, that put me inside that long-ago moment: "We stand there watching her burn. Well, George says, I hate to lose my pictures I had. And my bed. I don't give a damn much about the rest of it. Well, I says, I'll go get a team in, and we'll build you another one. You saved my goddamn Dutch oven. Oh, the hell with it, ol' George says, as long as you got a cabin, I don't need none."

As I listened, my hand was resting on the sun-warmed chimney rocks, which were, I realized, a kind of grave after all. Though I was impressed by George's Dutch oven rescue, captivated by his antimaterialism, charmed by the easy friendship between him and Fae, the photographs occupied my imagination above all; George's regret at losing the images over anything else he owned, as if they were the only emotional language he had.

I collected a cache of firewood—branches from a few fallen ponderosas strewn across the old homestead land—and then I undressed and scooted down an escarpment to the creek and jumped onto a flat, black rock. Silence and stillness. Then, the air moved. A creature with a thick coat curled its pliable body in and out of the rocks, shook water from its dark fur, sniffed, and pointed its nose in the air. Face pinched, foxlike, eyes blacking. I had no idea what animal I was seeing; only later, when I searched a field guide, did I identify him as a marten. But I believe not being able to name or scientifically classify him in the moment allowed me to regard him as a magical creature. We locked eyes, traded yellow throats. I can't say how long we stared at one another. A feeling passed through me. I had seen other wild animals, a cow and calf moose, a black bear, deer, elk, a wolf, but those encounters had been shadowy, and brief.

With the marten, I had time.

I'm no Annie Dillard, whose essay about the weasel I know well, but I felt the separation that afternoon, a self flowing out of myself, hovering over the water, landing on the dark rock, and slipping into the marten, felt his ticktock pulse, the instinct to run, heard an antler scrape a tree a mile away, the sound of hooves, saw him seeing me, then I traveled back into my own skin, to wonder and agitation mixed.

The creature seemed to be winking, holding up his palm. I was confused by the gesture. Was he communicating something? He rubbed his face, and I rubbed my cheek. He could have darted away. He stayed. And stayed. Until I quietly combed a lock of hair from my eyes. He let out a yikker then slithered under the rock and disappeared into the brushy bank.

I clung to the rock. Maybe he would return.

✢

So moving was the marten encounter for me, I once wrote about it for a class taught by a famous personal essayist from New York City, who had never stepped foot in a wilderness. He told me my essay was boring. That wild animal encounters were clichéd topics. At the time I felt withered by his criticism, but later I was grateful for the feedback, however rudely delivered, because it pushed me to figure out why that meeting on George's land was so important. I think it's because I learned that martens were persecuted animals, hunted almost to extinction at the same time I realized that George sympathized with persecuted people and may have felt maltreated himself.

Some papers I had already gathered related a story of George hiring an African American fire camp cook in 1931—the only African American I came across residing in the Selway-Bitterroot of that period, which I took to be significant during the shameful era of Jim Crow. The man may have taken the train from the South or Midwest to Lewiston. The city was a bustling center of activity in the 1920s and 30s, and he most certainly would have heard about Forest Service work during fire season. Whatever the case, when the cook arrived at camp after a three-day horse trip, a crew member asked if he could make doughnuts, a popular comfort food for soldiers in the trenches during World War I. "Man, you want doughnuts," the cook said, "you'll have doughnuts." According to the account, "He dropped large spoonfuls of dough into a 25-man boiler of grease and turned out puffballs the size of popcorn balls—two dishpans full in record time."

I couldn't locate the cook's name or determine what happened to him, which didn't surprise me since African Americans are routinely erased from the historical record of this country. What did surprise me is that I found another account stating that in the summer of 1940, during smokejumper training, George hired a Chinese cook at Moose Creek. When one of the white men, Earl Cooley, complained, using the racist tropes of dirty food and foreign manners to refer pejoratively to both the cook and George, George shrugged it off and kept the cook on staff. He only capitulated when Cooley threatened him. "I gave George five days to find a [new] cook, or I'd take the crew out of Moose Creek."

And then there was the ridge runner, a man as mysterious as a Yeti, though he has been written about by a number of local historians. What he looked like, no one knew. He crept around the woods like a marten, hiding in hollowed trunks or under rocks or in caves. From the 1930s onward, the Forest Service maintained log cabins stocked with supplies. The ridge runner made a key from a tin can reinforced with the broken blade of a jack knife. He used the makeshift key to enter cabins and help himself to the provisions.

Rangers who came upon the raided cabins found jam and peanut butter jars scattered on counters, ketchup and mustard spilled on the floor, every dish soiled or broken, stovepipes removed, and the walls blackened with soot. In 1942, several foresters believed the ridge runner to be Baldy Webber, wanted for attempted murder. They organized a manhunt and ambushed him around his campfire. Except instead of Baldy Webber they found a stunted man of five feet two wearing an old blanket, socks made from dish towels, and missing his front teeth. They concluded that the ridge runner, whom they identified as William Moreland, was fleeing imaginary enemies, ghosts that pursued him along the peaks and valleys of the Bitterroots.

George was ranger during some of the ridge runner's antics, but he defended the man against charges of theft, maintained his innocence and his sanity. No one else in the Forest Service at that time seems to have agreed with George. "I don't know why he thought the man was innocent," my mother said when she learned it, but she seemed as pleased as I was that her father hadn't demonized the man. Of all the stories of George's protection of persecuted people, his treatment of the ridge runner easily became my favorite. Maybe because Moreland was committed, like Esther, to the Orofino sanitarium and stigmatized as a madman.

⊕

I waited that day a good half hour for the marten to return. He didn't. So I reluctantly climbed down from the rock and shuffled up the bank. As I dressed, I noticed that the mountains seemed higher than when I'd first come. I saw how, just as every time I came to the wilderness, the trees and rivers and creeks and animals put you in your place. Fae's oral history put something in place for me, too. George's tangled identity—his love of image and narrative, his willingness to rush into fire for a friend, and his effort to defend the persecuted and take care of those who, like me, my mother, my grandmother, struggled with disordered mind states, moods that betrayed us or gave us power—was growing on me. I felt a separation, a self moving into George's experience, then back into my own skin, but changed. I even had a romantic notion to stay there for years like George did, making art, writing, communing with the animals, living skin to skin with the wild.

28 Big Trees Down

December 1, 2018

Fenn Ranger Station, gateway to the Selway-Bitterroot on the Idaho side. A cold November drizzle. Cookhouse filled with casseroles, green and potato salads, vegetable and meatball dishes, plump dinner rolls, and an amber note inside us all, building as we talk together. Fifty or so of us, shaking hands, hugging, eyes meeting, reaching deep to find what part of Connie we share.

Some of these people I've never met. We have name badges, but we blend into one fleece-jacketed, hiking-booted human being.

Anna, the current wilderness ranger, says, "I knew I had big shoes to fill when I took Connie's job after she retired."

Carol chimes in. "Big shoes," she repeats. "Connie taught me everything I know and love about wilderness, and now I've spent my whole life there."

"Connie loved the Selway-Bitterroot, and I love it, too, and to deal with her disappearance, I have to think she's become part of the land she loves," Mel says.

"There are still so many unanswered questions," Susan says.

Mel's not denying it. He's the one who hired Connie thirty years ago. "Sometimes I feel guilty for introducing her to this area," he says, "but I wouldn't take that away from her, despite everything."

I've driven to the memorial with Myron and Dick. Though Dick knows everyone, is his own kind of wilderness celebrity, he sticks with us. And I realize I want him to stay close by. When he wanders off, my eyes search the room, and I shuttle over to stand by him, feeling close to the wilderness itself.

"Connie was in camp totally alone," Dick says, almost an afterthought.

"Right after Lloyd died," Amy says, "she had to leave the farmhouse and she bought a place in Nezperce, in town."

I've seen Amy before. Blonde hair, tall, late thirties or early forties, emanates strength. She seems to wear the whip of the late autumn wilderness in her hair and cheeks. When Amy worked trail crew years earlier, I spent a night in her company at one of the ranger stations. I doubt she remembers me, but I can't help staring at her. She looks so much like Connie. A young Connie.

"Lloyd had a bunch of firearms in that farmhouse," Dick says.

"Why'd he have firearms?" I ask.

"He was law enforcement in California before he came up to Idaho. I don't know what she did with those guns when she moved into town."

"She wasn't happy in town," Amy says. "She put on a bright face for everyone, but inside, it tore her up."

"Candy and I've had conversations," says Dade. "Did she do it intentionally? We say no. She wouldn't have taken Ace. She wouldn't have signed on as a cook. It wasn't like her to let others down."

"Everyone I've talked to is real certain she didn't take her own life," Dick says.

People continue to fill plates, sit down, stand up, squat to talk to one another.

Soon, we head into another room, sit in assembly-like form, and people stand one at a time to speak. A young man in Carhartt overalls and a crewcut says, "The first time I met Connie, she'd backpacked to Moose Creek all by herself, that's twenty-five miles, and she was still doing it when she was really old. When I was going through outfitter's training, I shared a room with her. There were a bunch of firefighters and mule wranglers around, and she was there to work shoulder to shoulder with them. At her age, that's impressive. One night we were walking back to the bunkhouse together, I told her, *I hope you take this the right way, but sister, you got balls.*"

"I feel like I need to respond to this old woman shit," Chris says. He's standing, a towering man with a deep voice and silver spike earring. "We as a culture don't respect elders. The Lakota have a word for old woman, it means *wise one above.*"

"Boy was she a workhorse," says a man with a white swirl of hair over his bald head. "You couldn't say no to her." And I think of Connie bustling around the kitchen at Moose Creek, lighting lanterns, making tea, asking people about their lives.

"You didn't have to know her long to know how she worked," says Amy, "to know her rules: You don't unpack her mules, you don't *not* let her unpack yours; she's allowed to fuss over you, you're not allowed to fuss over her. And you do not chop Connie's wood—ever—in the wilderness or at home."

"You did what she told you," Chris says, wiping a tear from his eye. "She told me to quit yelling in the woods. I have a loud voice, but I quit for her."

"I'm just glad I never pissed her off," says Susan.

"She was relentless," says Carol. "She wrote grants, brought in all those volunteers from Iowa."

I recall all the times Connie told me about Iowa. She brought Iowa teachers and high schoolers to the Idaho wilderness under a grant she wrote called Reach a Teacher, Touch the World.

"She changed my life when I came as a teacher from Iowa," says Chris. "I miss her."

"I didn't even know her, never met her, but I miss her," says another man. "She's so real."

"If you met her once, or a few times, if you knew her for a year, or a few years, or thirty years," Ed says, "she gave the impression on that first meeting that you knew her your whole life, or some previous life, some kind of music inside you started humming, saying you'd always been part of her."

⌁

People grab dessert, file out to the bonfire, smiling, chatting, like people at a celebration, not like people who are mourning.

A quiet woman's voice behind me says, "Ace was a young dog. Not fully trained. Maybe he took off after an animal, and Connie sprinted after him, became confused, who knows."

"I think she went for a walk, and she got out on some ridge near a trail. There're talus slopes everywhere; I've slipped on talus slopes twenty miles north of there and almost killed myself," says Bob.

"I heard she left her day pack and real pretty Diamond Willow hiking stick at the camp," the quiet voice says.

"I just wonder," says Dick, "if it wasn't an animal."

"Decomposed granite, it's all over the place," says Bob, "tottering stacks of loose stones that clank and clink as they shift underfoot. It doesn't matter how much you know the country, talus is talus is talus, it moves, it's tricky. It always terrifies me when I walk a talus slope and look to my right at a thousand-foot drop. Even the most experienced wilderness person can put one foot on a little piece of talus, and *zzzzip*."

"I thought either a bear or wolf," says Dick. "But Ace. If it'd been a bear, the dog would've barked and scared it away, and a bear would not have killed the dog, unless the dog went up to the bear, which, if the dog had any sense at all, he wouldn't do. A wolf could kill a dog."

"I don't think it was wildlife," says Ed. "There'd have been ravens."

Myron says, "Did anyone find her car?" He wonders if she went back to get her car and drove off, creating a new identity.

"The car is accounted for," Dick says.

Mel says that, in 1990, he'd been going through his stack of applications. "These were mostly college kids looking for summer jobs, and then I came upon this Iowa schoolteacher looking to work summers in the forest. So I gave her a call, and her response was *Yes!* I remember the day she arrived. She walked into my office, it was like the first meeting of old friends. At the end of the summer, she said, *I don't want to go home. I've fallen in love.*"

"Connie and I were tight," Joe says on a taped message Anna plays. "I remember her coming to the old Seminole ranch to get away from pilots at Moose Creek, and you know how she liked her red wine. I remember it was a little bit of a ping-pong watching her walk across that swinging footbridge back to Moose Creek."

Laughter. We wander back to the assembly room.

Ed says, "After the wilderness ranger interns left one year, I said to her, once you spend a summer in the wilderness, you never come out all the way. She said, *That's why we do it, Ed.*"

"I was reading something she wrote in the Moose Creek logbook," Anna says. "If I can never come back here again, heaven forbid, I'm comforted that we who cherish wilderness are represented in future generations. Moose Creek will live on because of all of us who have loved it, and those who will continue. They will do it even better. Momma Moose, ex-wilderness ranger for a long time."

Someone's crying. It's Chris again. Bald head rose-red, gray T-shirt stained with tears. He's not even trying to hold back, seems to know he's big enough to weep for us all. Finally he blows his nose, gains composure. His sobs remain as an echo.

"I feel so lucky I got to see Momma Moose in her natural habitat at Moose Creek," says a young woman with curly auburn hair. "One time at a bonfire, I was sitting next to her, and she gave me this handkerchief. It says, 'A woman's place is in the wild.' I carried this all season, and when we were searching for her, I had it with me."

I stand up. "I've written something," I say, and I read about Connie and the disappearance of the Dog Creek Bridge, her exasperation, her patience with me. "Connie is my bridge into that strange and difficult place," I say.

"She created this community," Amy says with clear blue eyes. "She was Momma Moose. You'd come into Moose Creek tired from eight hours on a horse, or ten hours hiking a trail, and she'd take care of you. You belonged to her whether you knew it or not." Her voice wavers and she finds a clear note. "I guarantee everyone in this room, whether you knew her for five minutes or twenty-five years, she had adopted you. Once I was at Moose Creek, and she was making bread, cooking roast, getting people drinks, talking to them, telling them stories, taking care of everybody, and I said to her, *That is not your job.* It was one of the very few times I crossed her, and she looked at me, and she said, *It is my job. It is absolutely my job, and it's everybody's job to take care of one another. Don't ever tell me it's not my job.*"

Chris's tears flare up again. He and Connie used to love to lie on their backs and look at the sky. "She loved the stars, the stories of the heavens." He wipes his eyes, clears his throat, says there's a stump in the Bernard Devoto Grove, a big circular stump, and he goes there and lies on his back and looks up at the huge open circle where the tree used to be, but now he sees it differently. Connie's favorite song was a folk tune that asks who is going to hold up the sky now that the big trees are gone. "In October, for the first time, I saw in the canopy opening that big tree missing," he says.

"Because of the mystery, she'll remain a legend forever," Susan says, and I recall the time I heard someone arguing with Connie about George Colgate, the deserted cook of 1893. A cigar-mouthed guy with a red, wrinkled neck like a turkey snood said, "That stuff they got on that little wayside rest stop, down there at Colgate Licks, they got a grave marked out with rocks and a sign that says George Colgate died and was buried there. That's not true. George Colgate never died twelve miles of there. He was further downriver. Forest Service shouldn't put out stuff like that." Connie wouldn't hesitate to contradict people. Other times, she let criticism fly over her head like a gulp of swallows at dusk. She just smiled at this old-timer, handed him a cup of coffee, and said, "Oh, Dan," as if it was perfectly reasonable for someone to disappear in the Bitterroots and leave behind a tangle of mystery.

Again, Anna recites Connie's words, written five years earlier. "I yearn to go further into the hills, to those outer reaches along familiar streams and old campsites, the places that have taught me so much."

As we disperse, I search the pooling guests for Amy, make a beeline for her. "I have some notes from one of my discussions with Connie," I say. "She said you were like one of her daughters."

Amy smiles wide and gracious. We talk about Moose Creek, about being on trail crew, about what might have happened. Her eyes are damp as she tells me she was on Connie's search and rescue team. "They had a camp journal," she says. "On Tuesday, Connie wrote, *Rained all day, had to postpone the trip to Big Rock.* Wednesday morning she wrote: *Beautiful day, ground is frozen and crisp.*"

When the outfitters talked to Connie on the radio Wednesday at 3:00 or 4:00 in the afternoon and communication was poor, Amy went on, they now believe she was telling them she was hiking to Big Rock to check it out. It would have been a perfectly reasonable trip, only a mile and plenty of daylight. There was another clue to indicate that she left Wednesday and never returned. Ace had been jumping on her bed with his dirty paws. Connie had brushed off the bag and it was hanging outside. It rained Wednesday night, and when the hunters returned to camp Thursday afternoon, the bag was sopping wet.

I lean in, feel something opening, and then a hand reaches from behind Amy and pulls her away.

29 Tracks

I first comprehended how difficult it is to find lost things in the wilderness through Dick. Once, before a winter flight on which Dick let me tag along, he gave me a report, written some seventy-seven years earlier by my grandfather and another Forest Service employee, documenting their ski trip through the Selway-Bitterroot tracking a marten poacher named Boyd. Poachers like Boyd were the worst kind of outlaw because they hunted animals in winter at their most vulnerable time. Boyd was a loner, as I've since learned, one reason he was so difficult to capture. But he'd left a paper trail in Hamilton grocery stores and bars and made the sloppy mistake of dropping word of his plans with a waitress at the café. Maybe he was trying to impress her.

Wolverine tracks, 2009. Dick Walker photo.

On February 13, 1933, according to the report, George and his colleague drove from Missoula to Hamilton. Over a meal of beef stew and potatoes at the diner, they learned that Boyd had gone up Lost Horse Creek a day earlier. The two-man team drove to the mouth of Lost Horse Creek that evening, and the next day, they strapped on skis and their Trapper Nelson packs, each man carrying a bed, dried beef, bannock flour, butter, instant coffee, sweet chocolate, concentrated soup sticks, English walnuts and dates ground together, one pair of extra socks, matches, candles, a flashlight, a pocket compass, a one-man mess kit, a roll of adhesive tape, lace belting, a small hand axe, and ski wax.

My own pack was much simpler when I set out with Dick, who had been hired to document snowmobile trespassers for an environmental group. Snowmobiling in the wilderness is prohibited, just as all motorized transportation and tools are. But it's hard to catch snowmobilers on foot with snowshoes or skis. Flying overhead, Dick could spot their tracks. Dick had let me tag along because we would be tracing George's 1933 route in reverse.

I'd driven to Dick's house the previous night in a world of pain from menstrual cramps, thinking I'd be better in the morning, but when I woke up, fog lay thick and white as a bowl of glue across the valley. I felt delirious as I listened to Dick in the other room arguing with the flight weather service operator. He hung up and stomped around, talking to himself. "I'd rather fly in snow than fog. Even snow is bad, coming out on a prairie in snow is scary as hell when you can't see which way is up." I covered my head with the pillow. I had no business, I knew that, scrunching into a tiny plane and flying foggy mountains, but if I stayed home, I might never follow in George's footsteps on his manhunt for Boyd. So there I was on a cold February day in the airplane breathing into my pain at seven thousand feet and concentrating on the past.

February 14, 1933: At Lost Horse Creek, George and his partner skied a mile beyond the forest boundary in three feet of snow, slightly crusted, where they discovered a dim trail that led to a small trapper's cabin and human tracks. "As near as we could determine from examination of the snowshoe tracks, they wrote, they were from 2 to 3 days old, but due to recent snows we could not ascertain whether these tracks were headed up or down the creek."

I glanced up. Dick and I were flying east as the clouds cleared. McConnell Mountain and Grave Peak shot through the horizon. Dick told me that Grave Peak was a sacred Nimíipuu site, and also the setting for one of Norman Maclean's short stories based on time he spent as a lookout there in 1919. He'd read Maclean dozens of times and—along with other favorites like David James Duncan, Rick Bass, Terry Tempest Williams, Mary Clearman Blew, Wallace Stegner, and Gary Snyder—he could pluck entire passages from memory, just as he could passages from the Wilderness Act. "Know your watershed!" Dick would say, quoting Snyder.

The snowcapped peaks were delicate lace strips, one mountain silhouetted behind the other, like the frill of a petticoat. As we crossed the flat expanse of Kooskooskie Meadows, noded with stands of ponderosa pine, Douglas fir, and Western larch, I felt weightless. My pain seemed to be subsiding. Then: "Trespass!" Dick whispered into the noise-canceling headphones as he pointed out two parallel lines below—snowmobile tracks. It felt as if we'd just spotted enemy troops. He aimed his camera straight down and took rapid-fire shots while his knees steered the plane. "Those sons-a-bitches," he growled.

The ground was too white to face with bald eyes, and even with my shades, my eyes squeezed into slits. I didn't dare say so, but the snowmobile tracks seemed beautiful from this height, curving with the natural arches of the land, down a valley and up a mountain. White hills crusted in glitter. It was hard to think of them as the enemy.

❧

On February 15, 1933, George and his partner followed Boyd's snowshoe tracks for five miles until they found a small wikiup, fir branches leaned against a tree to make a shelter. Inside, fresh boughs covered the floor for a bed, along with a snuff can dated January 12 and a newspaper dated January 15. The headlines, a mix of war on sea and war on land, might have read: "China Holds Japan Army On Three Fronts," "Fire Sweeping Big Sur Woods," and "San Quentin Convict Slain by Fellow." The men sifted through a recent campfire and decided Boyd had built the wikiup not two days earlier. "We left following the snowshoe tracks till about 5:00 p.m. when on account of the fresh snow which had been falling all day we could no longer follow them," they wrote. "We traveled on until 7:00 p.m. and made camp for the night under a tree."

The next day, George and his partner continued tracking Boyd.

⟿

Though Dick and I were following George's path as we looked for snowmobile trespass, we were also searching for wolverine tracks, which, Dick said, we could see from the plane once the weather cleared. Wolverines and snowmobiles were connected. Snowmobilers, with their aggressive roars and looping paths, displaced wolverine families.

"Can you really see the tracks from the air?" I asked. Dick shrugged. A sharp stab in my abdomen took my breath away, and I gasped at the pain and because I never knew the right time to ask questions, when they were appreciated or when I was a bother.

But Dick welcomed my inquiry. "You'd be surprised how much you can see when the sun's out on the snow," he said. I imagined the wolverine, a thirty-pound beast in a powder-puff body and hybrid face—part cat, part dog, part human. I saw the female wolverine in her den, rattled by the high scream of the snowmobile, grabbing her kits and making a run for it, a refugee, the whole family vulnerable. Ironically, Dick said, when the mother flees her home, she uses snowmobile tracks as her own private superhighway, finds a secondary den and then, when she feels safe, returns home.

As he talked, hands safely back on the steering mechanism, I felt blood draining inside me, maybe in sympathy for the wolverine mother. "But if the high traffic keeps up," he said, "she and her kits become permanently homeless." As I conjured an image of the fleeing wolverine, I immediately saw George and his partner displacing Boyd, pawing through his vacated wikiup. Then I reminded myself that Boyd was the outlaw, the predator, killing the already overhunted martens, close cousins of the wolverine.

"There's some!" Dick said. We were flying across a saddle, but in the tree shadows and the snow glitz, nothing looked like animal tracks to me. Did I really know what wolverine tracks looked like? Wolverines, Dick told me, have plantigrade posture. They walk on the soles of their feet like humans. Five toes, inch-long claws, and a loping foot drag. I strained and squinted as Dick thrust his finger emphatically across my face to the windshield. "Right there, coming from that tree." He turned the plane and banked hard so I could get a second look.

Miraculously, I saw them. Running from the base of a tree for about twenty yards. In twos, skimming along the surface. So fragile, so complete, like perfect, tiny globes. They were truly beautiful, especially compared to the snowmobile lines. Then the tracks ended right there in the snow, as if the animal had vanished.

As Dick and I continued to trade information about the wolverine, I could see how the animal personified the mountain spirit of people like Connie, maybe my grandfather, and Dick himself. Wolverines stay in high country—the open land above the tree line. In the Bitterroot Mountains, high country comprises a narrow band about twenty feet wide along the rugged peaks where few animals can survive. Bears sleep all winter. Cougars and wolves descend to lower elevations to get away from the snow. I thought of the tenacious mother wolverine lugging her kits from her den while angry machines, snowmobiles and airplanes, thundered by, part of the pain of being born female.

My reverie was interrupted by the plane, which started teeter-tottering. There was nothing I hated more. And then, once again, pain stabbed at me, deeper this time. I loosened my seat belt and fingered my pack for Power Bars.

"You okay?" Dick asked.

"Yeah," I said, weakly.

"You're tough."

"Not really." I was trying not to throw up. "It feels like we're ascending and descending really fast."

"It's not the up and down. That might be what you sorta feel. It's the steep turns." He was turning, he said, to slow the aircraft. "The faster you're going in turbulence, the higher the magnitude of turbulence you feel, and once you get to a certain speed, each aircraft, depending on its weight, has what they call maneuvering speed, the speed at which you maintain the dimensional stability of the aircraft and not have it disintegrate."

"Right. I definitely don't want things to come apart." I looked at him, trying to understand what he'd just said, thinking, Am I going to be okay?

Dick pressed buttons and eyed the instruments. "The smartest thing to do if you're apt to be queasy is you get access to that cold air." He turned a metal vent onto my face. "Some people can't handle this. Can't handle the steep turns. I've had people puke!"

"What then?"

"You turn around and plain ol' ass-abort the whole fucking mess."

I focused on the cold hitting my face, air entering and leaving my lungs, and the hollow place in my back. Put the sickness there, I told myself. Don't fall apart.

↩

By February 17, George and his partner were contouring around a mountain. In and out of the draws they skied, following Boyd's tracks up to Twin Lakes cabin, but because of the thick snow, they couldn't get in. They knew of another trapper's cabin five miles down Moose Creek. At 1:00 p.m., they started off, thinking they could make that second cabin by nightfall. But as they skied down Moose Creek, darkness overtook them and, again, they camped under a tree.

The next day, they lost Boyd's tracks. I had expected the trip to end there, with their defeat, Boyd's tracks vanished in the snow. But the narrative took a surprising turn. On February 18, they wrote:

> A short ways from the camp we saw an otter track which was the first sign of game we had seen since leaving Missoula. We continued down Moose Creek to the mouth of Dead Elk Creek. There we back tracked about 1 mile and looked for a cabin which we had found Boyd using as headquarters in 1932. We were unable to locate this cabin, so we continued to the mouth of Jeanette Creek where we camped for the night in an old trapper cabin. However, there were no tracks to indicate that this cabin had been used at any recent date.

What had happened to George and his partner was a revelation: they lost Boyd's tracks, they even lost their cabin, but they found otter tracks. The otter was a crucial moment in their quest because right where the hunter's tracks left off, the hunted's tracks began. It reminded me that the line between difference, between humans and animals, is a very fine one. And I realized that I, too, was a tracker. Tracks and tracking are ways of following history and tracing ancestry as much as they are reading the land in the present.

After Dick stabilized the plane, my nausea subsided enough to ask him what excited him most about tracks: the marks themselves or the actual animals?

"Oh, it's both, it's both!" He talked about a time he skied up a drainage looking for a snow bridge to cross, and he saw tail-drag places and then tracks and then tail-drag, and then the marks just disappeared. "So you know what you're looking at are otter. The otter are swimming around, and there's a hole, and they dive down, and maybe they get some whitefish or a westslope cutthroat, and you can see the tracks. They're either going up or going down, because in the middle of whatever otters are doing, they always take time for a little recreation slide. Slide and dip, slide and dip. They slide down and go *whoop!* And they'll do it on their backs, they'll do it on their bellies, just like *eee-hee-hee-hee!* You know?"

My grandfather was no different. By February 19, 1933, he and his partner had completely given up on Boyd. Now, all they saw were animals:

> Left cabin at Jeanette Creek and traveled to Cougar Cabin where we saw a mountain goat on the south side of Moose Creek. From Moose Creek Falls down to this cabin, moose tracks were numerous. We were able to get within ten feet of a cow moose feeding in one of these channels when she saw us and ran up the creek and disappeared into a tunnel formed over the creek by drifted snow.
>
> February 21. We traveled down Moose Creek to Blum Ranch. The snow was fifty inches deep. A large number of old elk tracks, made probably a week before our arrival, were noted at the salt, but evidently the elk had moved back to the higher country. We wrote a note to our supervisor reporting our failure to connect with Boyd.

Tracking a poacher, tracking a trespasser, and tracking an animal in the backcountry easily bleed into one another; I see that now even better than I did on that winter flight with Dick. Just as George lost Boyd's story in the snow and found instead the tracks of otter, mountain goat, elk, and cow moose, Dick and I lost the snowmobile tracks but found the wolverine. I can't remember how our trip ended, can't recall the landing or what we said to one another by way of small talk, but I do know that as I drove away from the hangar, I was light-headed and light-hearted, and my pain was gone. George had become clearer to me, more personal, and I felt for the first time as if he and I were living rhymed moments, traveling parallel tracks that crossed now and then in unexpected ways.

30 Sustained

The trail of George and Esther's story—our story—seemed to come full circle when my mother went to the wilderness not as a tourist or as a voyager looking for completion but as an employee of the Forest Service, like Dick, like Connie, like her parents. Some ten years after Esther's death, she and my father started working as volunteers at the Shearer Guard Station, a position I helped them obtain through Connie. They went every fall for five or six years.

Shearer Station is fifteen miles up the Selway River from Moose Creek. It's smaller than Moose Creek—just an airfield, one cabin, and a tack shed. "Shearer's my favorite place," Connie told my parents when they signed up. "You don't get the same traffic as you do at Moose Creek. It's more intimate. More wild." During late September and early October, they would see a few hunters, a few firefighters and trail crew, and not many other people.

The last year they volunteered, they hiked in. They'd been there two weeks when Dick shuttled me to Shearer one clear afternoon for a weekend. My parents were waiting at the side of the airstrip when we landed. "How are you, young lady?" Dick said to my mother in a frisky tone as we got out of his plane. The two of them smiled at one another—my mother in her short dark hair with red bandana wrapped around her skull, Dick with his adventuresome Musketeer beard and mustache. Their playfulness didn't seem to bother my father. Both Dick and my mother flirted with everyone—men and women.

I wasn't surprised when Joe happened to be there. "I'm picking up some hunters," he said. "They should be here pretty soon."

The five of us stood on the edge of the runway, my mother chatting with Dick, my father with Joe. I was popping my head into one conversation and then into another when I heard Joe say, "Jared Diamond" in an authoritative voice.

"I know that name," I said.

He turned to me. Sunglasses shaded his eyes. "Have you read his book?" Everyone grew quiet.

"*Collapse*? Yeah, I've read it."

"Well, I'm not sayin' I understand everything he wrote," Joe said, "but I agree with him. We're ruining our planet, and it's gonna collapse."

"I have a theory about apocalypses," my father said, eyes moving rapidly, bouncing on the balls of his feet like a changeling, as if he could land this way or that on the issue of environmental ruin. "God did the flood once, but whatever he's got for his second shot is gonna be worse than the flood. Worse than climate change. Worse than cyclical collapse."

My mother smirked over Joe's shoulder. She seemed to be enjoying the mounting tension.

Then Dick stepped forward. "There's so much we don't fucking understand about what we're doing to these places." Dick's voice was heated, raw. I'd seen him get passionate many times, but this was directed at my father, and I felt a crashing inside of me. Both men wanted to be taken seriously, but my father was smiling impishly, almost daring Dick to do something irrational.

Dick stepped forward again and placed one hand on each side of my father's head, squeezing as if he were talking to an errant child. "Sustainability," Dick said sharply, voice rising. "Fucking sustainability."

The two old bucks were locking horns. Alarm shot from my mother's eyes.

I thought my father was going to haul off and hit Dick. I thought Dick was going to haul off and hit my father. Maybe they wanted to. I could tell my father felt humiliated, and angry, the way his face went slack.

"Dick," he said, releasing himself from Dick's grip, "see all these little sapling trees?" and he pointed to some spindly pines. "There's sustainability. See the older trees dying and the younger trees coming up? They're taking the carbon dioxide we're breathing out and producing oxygen— there's some more sustainability."

George Case, Selway-Bitterroot Wilderness, 1925. Family photo.

"That ain't gonna be here much longer," Dick said, once again moving toward my father, who braced himself. I braced myself, too, as the two men skidded toward violence. "We're using up way too much. It's all over!"

"Come on, you guys." My mother stepped between them, putting a hand on each man's chest and pushing them apart. My father fell back and laughed sheepishly. Dick turned and strode off to cool down. I stood amazed. And hugely relieved. My mother had taken control as if this were her place. As if she made the rules.

That night in the Shearer cabin, huddled around the table, we ate salmon and zucchini. My father made tea. While my mother and I washed and dried dishes, Dick and my father sat near the stove without speaking.

"I love being at Shearer," my mother said, placing a plate in the rinse water. "I've needed this. I lived a lot of my life, maybe my whole life, in my sister's shadow. My parents thought she was perfect. Barbara was the darling of the wilderness. I'd seen photos of her here. I always thought if I could come here, I could capture some of that."

I retrieved a dish from the rinse pan. The sharp edges of her face, of her story, glowed in the lantern light. I thought of her sleeping under the car at Lost Horse as the phantoms of George and Barbara walked into the woods. She talked as if she were strong. But I could feel her fragility. The fragility we all have when we're left out, excluded.

"One year when Barbara was out here with Mother and Dad, she had to go to the dentist. That was after Dad and the crew built the airstrip. They flew Barbara to Hamilton and back all by herself."

"I saw that!" In George's movies, a few clips showed Barbara, a girl of four in a plaid skirt and bobby sox, climbing out the side hatch of a Ford Trimotor and into Esther's arms.

"Oh, how Mother pined away. She was sick with worry that it would crash."

"Barbara was fine, wasn't she?"

"The thing was, Mother always told that story in an aching way. It was the narrative of Barbara that got to me. Barbara, the child Mother yearned for. She had a spell over Mother. She was the sun casting her rays on Mother and Dad. I was left in the shadows."

My mother laughed quietly, almost shyly, hands busy in the soapy water. "I've needed to experience what she and my parents experienced. They had something I didn't. The Selway River, the Bitterroots—they were so close to St. Maries, a few hundred miles, but they were so far. I couldn't come back here while Mother was still alive. She thought she hated this place. She was my mother, and I would never have caused her that pain."

I was beginning to see something that had been invisible to me. For my mother, what was hiding in the wilderness was the ghost of Barbara, her spotlit place in the family. My mother's struggle between exile and belonging, George and Esther's emotional remoteness, Esther's mental illness, George's confused identity, the threads I'd been following for more than a decade, had been reduced for my mother to Barbara's inclusion in the wilderness and my mother's exclusion from it.

"I'm so sorry, Mom." I squeezed her wrist and a brief smile moved across her face.

The next morning, my mother and I washed laundry on the front porch. She scrubbed vigorously on a corrugated metal washboard, her black-and-gray hair lifting with the breeze. I rinsed and hung clothes—a couple of T-shirts and our underpants and bras—on the railing.

"We hiked up to Eagle Rock last week," she began. Eagle Rock is an arête towering above the station with a bald eagle's craggy face. I pictured my parents, healthy seventy-year-olds, strolling hand in hand up a trail lined in sword fern, hawthorn, and alder, river flowing endlessly below and clouds unfurling overhead.

"We were sitting under an elderberry bush," she continued, "and out of the corner of my eye I saw movement. It was a bear. About fifty feet away. We sat there real quiet for a long time. It wound its way along the contour of the mountain and pretty soon it stopped, sniffed, and sat on its haunches and just looked at us. It was small. It didn't have its mom, so it was probably two years old. First year by itself, I'd guess."

"I wish I could meet a bear," I said. The Selway-Bitterroot has one of the country's largest black bear populations, yet I'd only seen one. Bathing in a pool along the river, it paddled and splashed and then lumbered up a rocky embankment. When it was out of sight, I took off my clothes, plunged into the pool and splashed with my own paws, imagining I could absorb the power of its summer days, the dreams and auguries of its hibernation.

"Every time we hike to Eagle Rock, the bear's there. I know bears are wild creatures," my mother went on, "but I like to think it's waiting for me—"

We both looked up. A man was walking toward us.

At first he looked like a man—tall with long strides. As he got closer, I could see how straight his back was, how open his face. He was young.

"I bet it's that kid," my mother said. Her nose flared. She stiffened and lowered her voice. A few days earlier, she said, he and his friend had flown in, come up to the cabin with their rifles, and asked my mother if she'd seen any bears. She lied and said she hadn't.

The railing where I had spread our laundry hit the young man at eye level. His eyes, big and bright, sat extremely close together, separated by a rocky nose. He wore camo and a black ball cap. My mother greeted him with backcountry small talk, asking how his hunt was going. He looked at us through our underwear, bras, and socks as he talked. I stifled a smirk, but people let it all hang out in the wilderness.

"I just shot a bear," he said. I felt a jolt, as if I were entering one of my mother's tales, as if I were witnessing and playing a part in its unfolding just as I had as a girl in the grocery store parking lot with my brother on my mother's hip. This time, instead of resisting the unfolding, I trusted it.

The young man rubbed his hands up and down his thighs as if he were trying to generate some heat. Except it was already very warm out. He was worried about something—and that worried me.

"Well, let's see it!" my mother said, bolting up. We marched down the airfield, and as we neared the young man's camp in a stand of trees, the smell of bear came to us, deep, skunky, like musty urine, like a pigsty, like a dumpster full of rotting vegetables.

The bear hung by its bloody flanks from a high bar wedged between two firs. All flesh and muscles, it looked eerily human. The young man had made a mess. The severed head and hide lay in the grass, black and glistening. Nausea swept through me as I stood, arms crossed, in front of the skinless, vulnerable body. Metallic green and blue flies buzzed around insanely. Two rifles lay on the ground.

"*Oooh*, a small bear," my mother said, hands clasped behind her back, a glint of recognition in her eyes. My worry dissolved into a slow panic. Where would her attachment to the animal lead us?

"How old are you?" she said.

"Eighteen," he said. His eyes oozed earnestness, brows melting into his unlined forehead. There was innocence in him. But that didn't excuse him. I'd seen my father and brothers and Myron hunt deer, but they did so with respect: they used bows and arrows instead of rifles, knew how to care for meat, and took only what they could eat. This young man appeared to have done it for sport. I wanted to tell him off, except I was with my mother. I would follow her lead.

"Where do you live?" she asked. Her questions were penetrating, bold, and the young man offered information willingly.

"Hamilton," he said.

"With your family?"

"Got my own place."

A young man in the same position as the bear he'd killed—my mother's point. She studied the animal's body as if scrutinizing a sculpture in a museum. "That's a fine bear," she said. I was surprised. I thought she might grab his shoulders, shake him, scold him, or at least throw him some aggressive silence. Instead, she touched her hand to the animal's shoulder. "You know, the flies'll blow it if you don't get it in a cooler right now. See those flies?"

The young man's eyebrows perked up.

"They'll lay their eggs in it," she said. "Maggots."

"No, they won't," he said. I could tell by his voice he wanted to sound authoritative, but he didn't. His worried, darting eyes told me he was scared now that he'd killed the bear.

"You put that bear in the ice chests right now." Her voice was as raw as if it had come from the bear itself.

Two oversized coolers were stationed nearby. The young man snapped to attention, spreading a blue tarp under the bear and loosening the pulley. The corpse fell in a surprisingly graceful way.

"You put the hide in the cooler, too."

"Yes, ma'am," and he grabbed his knife.

"That's right," she said. Then, taking it from him, she tenderly showed him how to cut the bear into pieces while I stood by, a silent witness, cringing at the scrape of knife on bone. He kept looking up at my mother, maybe for affirmation, maybe for forgiveness, and I saw the young George, who'd shot his own bear. I saw that whatever my grandfather had done to hurt her, she had already forgiven him. In that moment, I felt intense admiration for my mother, saw her as a person separate from me, but also deeply entangled with my being. Those rocking chairs that my father had bought us the day I was born stopped swinging between remoteness and a desire for intimacy. And I realized, with a suddenness that leaves me astonished to this day, that the wilderness that had excluded us had also given us a sense of belonging.

When I think of that day now, I remember what the constellation facilitator at the retreat center said about epigenetics. Based on tests done with mice, neurologists and molecular biologists theorized that extraordinary experiences and traumatic events change genes on a cellular level. Those changes are passed to offspring. My mother could handle young hunters and their meat and old men and their opinions. The lessons of the Selway-Bitterroot Wilderness wound through her body just as salmon DNA coiled in the rings of fir trees.

If my mother and I were the kind of people who hugged, who said I love you and gazed into one another's eyes with sentimental tears, we would have done so as we walked back to the cabin. But at that point in our journey toward reconciliation, we didn't need to. Though never stated outright, our shared openness and generosity was implied, sensed, held. Whatever trauma and confusion our ancestors had passed down to us, they had also bequeathed a place in which we could finally understand one another. Later that night, I lay on the porch in my sleeping bag watching the half-moon rise. Elk Creek, the small stream flowing next to the cabin, sang. A bat chittered and stars loomed over the dark split in the mountain where the Selway flowed.

I woke the next morning to giant boulders bobbing their heads out of the low water of the Selway. The timothy grass of the airfield was covered in beads of dew. Other plants had lost their petals and leaves, life giving way to senescence. Inside, a roaring fire was taking the chill off the cabin and my mother was making pancakes. My father and Dick sat by the wood stove talking quietly about the silliness of Forest Service rules, a subject they could agree on. Two white-haired men, mugs in hands, their love of the land as strong as their coffee.

31 Boyd Lake

Cindy, the Nez Perce National Forest archaeologist, gave me a photograph of George standing between two giant loaves of snow in the Bitterroots. His tiny figure was a smudge in a haze of white. Apparently, the photo documents a third and final attempt to catch Boyd. A caption on the back reads:

> George and I snowshoe 22 days without a stop to try to catch Montana poachers on the Idaho side of the divide. Followed them to their cabin, but they were not there. Snowshoed to Twin Lakes cabin where we found Boyd Gifford. He pleaded guilty. So we took him by railroad to Missoula. Gave him 30 days. We spent 30 hard days catching him.

According to Forest Service papers, George named a lake after Boyd, the marten poacher, who led him deep into the woods where human prints turned to animal tracks. I didn't understand why George would name a landmark after an elusive criminal. But when Dick reminded me that the lake isn't on any map, I realized what George may have been saying: Some things can't be seized. Some things should remain a mystery. Dick called this kind of experience "being absorbed."

"Wilderness has her way with you," Dick liked to say. "She reveals and she conceals."

"I'm going to go to Boyd Lake one day," I would say. Since then, I've thought better of it. Boyd Lake has remained a mystery. Other things have become clear. For instance, that the language of wildness lives in the stories recycled through the landscape, in the energy left by people who have marked it—built on it, made a trail, witnessed a marten washing itself on a rock or elk tracks in the snow. I've come to know in my bones that protecting the wilderness is about much more than preserving natural environments. It is an ecology of stories that connects us all.

George Case, Selway-Bitterroot Wilderness, 1934. Courtesy of Dick Walker Historic Photo Collection.

32 Fog Mountain
May 1–2, 2019

Along the Selway River at Gedney Creek, where I camped the previous autumn, I find the triangular campsite lined with firs and pines. A mackerel sky. This time of year, it takes the sun a long time to sink behind the mountains.

I've come here to feel close to Connie. Even though I'm still thirty trail miles from where she disappeared at Big Rock, I'm closer here than I can be at home surrounded by furniture and a tidy lawn, by pavement and boxes from Amazon and the throb of the Internet. The air smells fresh. I notice how old man's beard, strung like a minty garland, has taken over branches that have died during the winter. Dozens of them have fallen on the ground. The decay has started and will end only when the leaves, lichen, and wood become the rich soil from which the roots grow, and then begin again. Cycles.

The small tasks of pounding stakes, chopping firewood, boiling water are a comfort. After making camp, I walk to the Fog Mountain gate where I'd seen the Missing poster last October. It's gone.

Back at my campsite, I wonder: What does it mean that a person is missing? The sign's disappearance means that I'll never pass this old road again without seeing Connie's face. But then, I've seen her likeness in other places, too. The interrupted conversation with Amy at the memorial stayed with me all winter. I kept filling in details about the rescue effort, imagining events that may or may not have been true, and kept working my way back to Amy. I had to hear her story. So I drove to her house twenty miles north of Spokane. A blustery March day. We were easy together right away, though we hardly knew one another. But then, her house had a warm, friendly feel. Big farm kitchen, huge windows, a dog curled in the corner, photos of her two boys on the fridge. She made ginger tea, and we sat at her table overlooking a forest, ten acres she and her husband owned. She, in jeans and blue sweatshirt, blonde hair tied back, seemed perfectly placed.

I reminded Amy I'd ridden Connie's mule Amy Anne, her namesake. I told her how I'd learned about Connie's disappearance. I read from an oral history I'd made of Connie years earlier: "I don't remember ever being afraid of anything in the wilderness. I'm a spiritual and faithful person and there's God taking care of me." I added, "She said she had the sense that the wilderness would always take care of her."

Amy opened up as if the story of Connie inside her couldn't be contained. "When I found out she went missing," she said, "I dropped everything." Her mother-in-law came to stay with her sons, and she departed immediately. She said she wasn't in the same physical condition as when she had worked trail crew ten years earlier, a reality that concerned her slightly. "All I knew was I had to show up in the wilderness."

She arrived at the small airport in Hamilton the same time as a guy from Wyoming with his bloodhound. "The man had met Connie only once. That was my first glimpse at how people were coming out of the woodwork for her," she said. Standing there with the backcountry pilot and Mr. Wyoming and his bloodhound, she felt suddenly small. "They were looking at me like, *What's this fat housewife doing here?*" She laughed, even though it was not a laughing matter. When the plane landed at Moose Creek, Amy didn't know what to do. The Moose Creek ranger, a man whose name she couldn't recall, asked who she was, what she was doing there. Mr. Wyoming handed her a dog collar. "He had so little faith in me, he told me to take the dog collar if I went anywhere because it had a GPS tracker in it. He took off for Big Rock, and I thought, fuck you, I'm not taking a dog collar. You have no idea I lived back here ten years.

She slipped behind the station to the outfitter camp. "It was so dark there, so depressing, I couldn't stay," she said. "Back in the office, I rifled through the maps. The ranger looked at me with a grimace, totally confused. He still had no idea who I was. I grabbed a map and said, *I promise I'll bring this back before I leave the woods*. He seemed very concerned for my welfare, said something about me leaving Moose Creek and never being seen again. Everyone was on edge. There was a sense that if Connie could go missing, anyone could."

While at the outfitter camp, she remembered that Connie loved Shissler Peak, so she decided to make a quick trip to Shissler, five miles straight up to a lookout, then loop around and hike down Half Way Creek, twelve miles in all. She packed food, a first-aid kit, and matches in her daypack, fully intending to come back to Moose Creek. As she took off, the ranger raised his skeptical eyebrows.

"I got up to Shissler saddle," she said, "and I thought, Whew, that was hard. I stood there at the saddle looking at the trail up to Shissler Peak, the trail back down to Moose Creek, the trail to Big Rock."

Then Amy went silent, pausing at the fork in the path, the fork in the story. I'd been hanging on her every word, felt the quiet unfolding of the narrative as if I had been there, as if I were co-creating it, as if we were both making sense of Connie together, which, I realize now, was presumptuous of me, because Amy had an intimacy with Connie I could barely fathom. Amy's chin lifted and her eyes half closed. A crow landed on a stump outside the window, and the dog jumped up. She took him back to his bed, and when she returned, she was crying.

"I literally couldn't go back, could not turn around and go to Moose Creek, to that dead, dark outfitter camp behind the station. I didn't know if I could make it to Big Rock. I thought briefly, I should go back and get my tent and sleeping bag, because I only had my daypack. It was 10:30 a.m., late. October days were short and getting shorter. It was fourteen miles to Big Rock. I'd never been to the camp, had no idea where it was. But I had to go."

It was a hard trail, steep, a solid climb, and she had to stop often, check the map, count the drainages.

"Finally I made it to Big Rock," she continued, "and I thought, Where's camp? I walked onto the ridge looking for the white outfitter tent or maybe some smoke. Nothing. I had about an hour until dark, and I realized I didn't have any idea what direction to go. The outfitter had some mules grazing up there, so I meandered with the stock. About twenty minutes till dark, I fired three shots with my pistol. No answer. So I said, It's time to make camp."

❦

I'm plopped in a lawn chair next to my fire reading the notes I've taken during my visit with Amy when I see lights bobbing behind Fog Mountain gate. I jog over, flashing my headlamp.

Two men on a double passenger ATV, dressed in full camo gear and bright orange vests, buzz to a stop.

Both have big beards, one blond, one red.

I say, "Where are you from?" Big rifles are strapped to the front of the ATV, big scopes and smaller guns slung over their shoulders, big binoculars around their necks. Their rifles are covered in camo patterns too, as if the purpose of coming to the Selway is getting geared up, to blend in so the animals can't know them. As if.

The smaller, blond one, is driving. He glares, and I realize I've been shining my headlamp into his eyes. "Oh, sorry!" I say and point it to the ground.

The bigger one, Red Beard, says, "Ohio," defensively, and I sense I'm more threatening to them than they are to me. Maybe my comfort in this place, my comfort in my own skin, scares them. Or they're hiding something.

"Ohio, great!" I say, trying to bring some ease into the moment, realizing I don't want them to drive away. I'm angling for a favor. Maybe they can transport me to the top in the morning. I know I can't get to Big Rock from Fog Saddle this time of year, but I can at least see across the landscape, wander down a trail, feel a little closer to Connie. I have some cash, can pay them for their trouble.

"Did you make it to Fog Saddle?" I ask.

Red Beard pipes up. "No, only halfway." He seems to relax. "We encountered snow six miles up."

We converse about what a severe winter it's been. I ramble on about the university closures, the treacherous roads, the endless days of bleak, and he seems to open up. "We brought our chainsaw up yesterday and removed some of the trees across the trail. We had to move rocks. It's a rough road, washed out. That's why they don't let full-sized vehicles up there."

Six miles. I've been up the road before. I don't want to be dropped at a snowline in the dark of the road. I won't ask.

"We chased a bear across the snow yesterday," Blond Beard says, as if he can't restrain his excitement any longer.

"Wow," I say, imagining them leaping from the ATV and post-holing through the sticky snow.

"Anything for a bear," says Red Beard.

I cringe.

"We came up today, thought we'd see him. We've looked everywhere. We must have scared him."

"Yeah, you must have."

They take off just as swiftly as they've come, new gear and all, and I think of the bear George shot captured in the photo from 1925, of the bear the boy shot at Shearer, of what it means to be a woman in the woods as opposed to a man. There are differences. I've felt them, lived them. Amy striking out alone in search of Connie; young men and their bear hunting. But the typical generalizations don't always hold up here. Connie working shoulder to shoulder with men, jumping from airplanes, bucking logs. Henry Pettibone baking bread, sewing, mothering his disabled brother Rufus and Martin Moe. Maybe that's the point. Here, men are free to nurture, women free to lead, roles break down as the necessities of survival flare up.

Back at camp, I make tea and toss more wood on the fire.

⇔

"When I was up on Big Rock," Amy had said, "I found three subalpine firs and made a fire. I crawled under those trees in my cotton hunting pants and waterproof jacket." She rose and grabbed more tissue, filled our tea mugs. Something shivered inside me. I have camped in snow, in driving rain, on the edge of precipices, but always with others to help, always with a tent or sleeping bag.

"Just to be where Connie was," she said, sitting down again. "By now it was day five. It had rained. It had snowed. I was just hoping that whatever happened to her was quick. I lay there. And I remember at twilight, watching the clouds come over the Crags, I thought, I love it here. I love it. And I talked to Connie. 'You love it, too. And if you had to go, I'm glad it was here.' I poked my head out at midnight, and the snow was coming down. I got up and gathered some more wood. I was on a nearly bald mountaintop at eight thousand feet in October. But I was in the most protected spot. Honestly, I was being watched over.

"In the morning, I woke up and it'd snowed two inches. It took a while to find the trail. And I thought, son of a bitch, the ranger at Moose Creek is going to call search and rescue on me. That's terrible! To take the search away from Connie would be the worst possible thing. I headed down the ridge. About half a mile later here come three search and rescue volunteers. They look at me like I'm a phantom, like I appeared out of nowhere, like who would be on the top of a mountain at seven in the morning? I said to the volunteers, *Please tell me you're not looking for me!* They said, *Who are you?* I told them, and they pointed me to the hunting camp, which was now a search and rescue camp. When I got there, I didn't want to be in the way, didn't want to be a burden, didn't want to be another mouth to feed, didn't want anybody worried about where I was going to sleep, so I took over Connie's job. I became the camp cook."

When Amy finished her story, I felt we—all who knew Connie—were linked in mysterious ways. I didn't say this. Instead, I remarked, "You resemble Connie, I've always thought so."

She smiled, eyes still damp. "Yeah, but I'm a little taller."

⌑

When I arrived at the Gedney Creek campsite earlier today, it was cloudy, but now, with the fire burned out, I stare past the old firs and young ponderosas. It's a new moon; the stars are layered into a deep night sky, no light pollution, no technology pollution except head lamp and paper notebook.

Connie loved the stars, the stories of the heavens. I pull my mattress and bag from the tent so I can sleep under the stars, recalling what the two bearded men had said: "You'd better have something warm to sleep in, because it got down to twenty-five degrees last night." But I'm toasty. I find Ursa Major, Orion, Cetus.

Next morning, the rock I'd perched on last autumn is covered in white water. River energy bubbles up in full force. Branches, logs, twigs, and peat moss, inch-high and tufted onto rocks, a thousand, thousand forms in pale and dark greens and earthy browns. The more I distinguish each separate thing, the more entangled they become. There's so much here the body loves, so much complexity the mind is drawn to, the need for the digital world completely disappears. That must have been one aspect Connie loved, what Amy loves. The more often you come, the more quickly you drop the numbing urges of the front country.

Amy had described Big Rock as an open space, downed logs, sparse subalpine firs, and trails everywhere because of the stock. Easy to lose your way at the base of the last hill. "Apparently Connie had a piece of tissue in her pocket, and she had tied it onto a tree to mark the trail," she explained. "Fifty feet up the hill, she'd put a cross of sticks. So when you're standing at the cross, you can see the tissue and find your way back down to the trail. The tissue was still there after Connie disappeared. If she would've come back down that trail, she would not have left the tissue. To leave any evidence of human impact is against everything she believes in. She didn't come down that way. That's not a guess."

A hummingbird appears, hovers for a nanosecond, bright blur of amber, then is gone, slipped into the ether. A spider, large brown body and white streaked across its back, perches on a rock. My shadow falls on it, then it vanishes. Nature is sudden, a bolt, shows itself in flashes and flickers.

The magnitude of the place widens the imagination; that's what Connie had been getting at all these years, what she pointed to and partially expressed. If you're able to define wilderness, to pin it down, then that isn't wilderness. Connie had a mind big enough to help people understand that their relationship to that undefinable thing was the most important one they would ever have. But for her, wilderness was more than just an individual against the roaring wild. It was deep community, a melding of old-timers and newbies, plants and animals and rocks and water and wind, always changing. People come to the wilderness with what they have—a box of wine, fresh tomatoes, huckleberries, encounters with bears, information about weather, questions, loss, madness, stories—and it's always enough.

Over the years, I've learned the trails of the Selway-Bitterroot well, have come to know the sound and the silence, the scent of fresh hanging in the air, the gossamer web shining against a wind-blasted peak, the stirrings these things create, and I believe in the deep meaning of this place. Yet something in me has wanted to release the pull of this land. I want to love it, but I don't want to consume it or let it consume me.

33 The Knowing Field

Two weeks later at a building on Fulton Street in Chicago, I was greeted by a white-haired man with an attractive hand-me-down look holding a giant cigar. Actually, it was a sage smudge.

"Can I touch you?" he asked. I nodded, and he wiped down my legs, arms, hands, head, told me to leave everything behind, meaning my mental baggage.

Inside, exposed brick and cinderblock walls. Hardwood floors. Twenty-three people—nine men, fourteen women—were assembled in a neat circle.

I had begged Myron to come along. Though he let me know he would rather have been at a Cubs game, he obliged. We took our seats in the

Milky Way, Selway Lodge, Selway-Bitterroot Wilderness, 2019. DJ Lee photo.

circle, and he sat with his skeptical head bowed, hands folded and tucked between tensed legs. Then Barry, the constellation facilitator, in casual shirt, jeans, and black sneakers, talked about epigenetics, inheritance, generations, the power of ancestors, and Rupert Sheldrake. Barry's parents were Holocaust survivors. "When your parents have been through the brutality of one of the most gruesome genocides in history, you have a lot of issues," he said. Myron relaxed in his chair, and I sensed his incredulity inching toward interest.

Barry explained that we would connect to our ancestors, that through a shared energy he called *the knowing field*, we'd discover what must be seen, what could be left behind, and what we could honor.

Then he invited people to sit next to him to start their constellation. A woman from Saint Croix volunteered. Her story was deep, a conflict between her warring ancestors—African slaves, native Caribs, and French colonialists. Dark hair pulled into a bun, in a jean skirt and linen blouse, she called on three individuals from the circle: one to represent slaves, one native Caribs, and the third a French priest. "This is a big story," Barry said, choosing more people from the circle to symbolize historical movements and ideologies. Island culture. Corrupt governments. Lost potential. The structural mechanism that causes people to war.

I was mesmerized. I'd never seen anything like it, and I felt myself expanding internally, but Myron stiffened and burrowed into himself. I could see he didn't want any part of the re-enactment, which didn't surprise me. I had a hard time coaxing him to the occasional yoga class. Barry abruptly tapped me on the head and led me into the center of the circle. "You're the blood that connects us all," he said. I reclined on the floor, contemplating the idea of blood connection while the others re-enacted the history of colonialism. Fifteen minutes later, the woman's insight emerged: "Most of us carry the blood of the oppressor and the blood of the oppressed in our veins. Warring ideologies pulse through our psyches," she said.

Throughout the next few hours, I was amazed at how unguarded we strangers became, in the way you can open up to someone you've never seen before and will never see again on a train or airplane because of the shared and prolonged physical intimacy of modern transportation. But because this was a communal and an ancestral scene, the intimacy felt deeper, longer lasting. People rose, told their stories. There was laughing, shouting, dying, cursing, crying. We represented family members or abstractions like God and Death. Secrets were exposed and traumas explored—rape, incest, suicide, divorce, abandonment, illness. Ancestors were heard, acknowledged, and released.

"There's a piece of land in Idaho and Montana," I said when it was my turn. "It's a wilderness." From their blank faces, I understood that most of my urban companions didn't know what a designated wilderness was. I mentioned no roads, no electricity, no vehicles. I said, "Millions of acres of trees and mountains. You get the idea." I told them about Esther's box, that I'd been traveling the land for fifteen years, and I couldn't stop. "I love the Bitterroots with everything I am, don't get me wrong. The wilderness needs to be protected, but I need to let it go."

Without missing a beat, Barry asked me to choose people to stand in for Esther, George, and the Wilderness. I singled out a red-headed woman from Bulgaria to play Esther, a pleasant-looking Russian to play George, and a striking woman from Chicago with bone-blonde hair to be Wilderness. The woman from Saint Croix stepped forward to represent me, and any resistance I had to this strange process gave way to something I can only describe as trust in my inner senses.

The re-enactment began. "I'm feeling very lonely," the redhead playing Esther said, collapsing to her knees in the center of the room. On the periphery, Wilderness spread her arms wide, chest tilted to the ceiling, her long hair hanging like a waterfall. Wilderness and George fell to the ground curling into one another, and I did a double take at the odd juxtaposition. I was seeing my grandfather make love with the land at the same time I was aware I was really just watching a pretty blonde Chicagoan and an amiable Russian awkwardly holding hands.

I swallowed my skepticism and went with it.

In the center of the room, the Esther-character grew more and more dejected, bent her head, wrung her hands. There may have been actual tears running down her face.

I was tempted to mention Esther's institutionalizations to Barry and the Bulgarian playing Esther. But I didn't want to control the narrative. I wanted to see what happened without my direction. Neither did I talk about my research at the Cherokee County Genealogical-Historical

Society, though it crossed my mind, how I had come across one of George's newspaper articles called "The Blues" buried amidst larger news about the war in Europe into which he would soon be drafted. "Depression," he wrote as a seventeen-year-old, "is caused by a lack of faith in the ultimate purpose of life, and exceedingly harmful to yourself and those about you." Although it went against my logical thinking, I had regarded George's article as a premonition, because twelve years later, he married Esther, and twelve years after that, she went to bed and wouldn't get up.

"How is your mom involved in all this?" Barry asked.

"She didn't feel entirely loved," I blurted out, although I had never really thought of her life in such terms before. "She was excluded from the wilderness until after my grandmother died."

Barry popped up and tapped a tall Hungarian woman wearing a blue silk shawl to be my mother. The woman had a graceful, feline gait as she strolled past George and Wilderness, throwing them an evil look, and then kneeled beside Esther. "It's just us, Mom. We have each other," she said in a cool voice so convincing I half believed they were my mother's words. Esther turned away, but this woman playing my mother placed her hands on Esther. "I love you, Mother," she said.

Suddenly, a flash of lightning, a crack of thunder. I jumped in my seat, incredulous. It was a typical Chicago thunderstorm, yet it seemed as if the heavens were responding. Barry looked at me with raised brows. "There are no coincidences in constellation work," he said with a smile.

Wilderness reached her arm across the floor, trying to pull Esther and my mother away. "I'm your mother, I'll sustain you," Wilderness whispered as a kind of taunt. Barry, meanwhile, walked the circle like a circus master. He beckoned forward a woman with shining eyes who gave the impression of a silver mirage in the desert. He placed her behind Esther, saying "This is Esther's mother."

"Mary," I said. "Esther was twelfth of thirteen children."

"Twelve," Barry said. "That's a long way to the mother," and I registered the subtext, the remoteness of maternal love.

I was in the midst of an unfolding narrative I was helping to create, but this time, because of all the kind souls helping me, I felt supported.

I watched in a kind of awe as Wilderness continued to wiggle her delicate fingers toward the women in the center of the room, saying, "I'm your mother" while also holding George. She was a nurturer and a temptress. Turning my eyes to the Bulgarian playing Esther—wearing a citrus-orange dress, a carnation-pink sweater, and leggings patterned with daffodils, sitting stoically—I realized that my grandmother was not the spider at the center of the family web but a fruiting, flowering power.

All of a sudden, I felt tired of the narrative, and I searched for my mother. It was *her* role that concerned me above all. Of course, the woman playing my mother was the one holding everything, everyone, together—Esther, Mary, George, the land, and me. The woman from Saint Croix walked around the circle, eyes wide and unblinking, just like my own.

⊷

"That was actually kind of cool," Myron said as we left the building.

"Really?" I was surprised. Though I could see he'd been paying attention, I hadn't known if he was simply enduring the workshop for my sake.

"You know what I got out of it?" he said, raising his slightly graying brows. "Esther may have felt alone in the mental asylum. She may have felt alone in the wilderness. Actually, she was surrounded by love. She felt compelled to the land because George was there, and it was trying to hold her. But her daughter was hugging her. Her mother was hugging her. Her granddaughter was there. Esther was more loved than the land. She was the center of everything."

It was more insight than I had gleaned. As we motored through the streets in silence, all I could think about was how, at the end of my constellation, George said, "I love the land more than I love them," how Barry lined up the women, Great-Grandmother Mary, Esther, my mother, the representative of me, and me, each with our hands placed on one another's shoulders, my own hands stretched toward an imaginary Steph and whoever would come after her, and how Barry said, "You can let the land go, but it's there for you, always." How the thunderstorm that had been building outside finally burst and rain hammered the metal roof to drive home the point.

⊷

A few nights later, Esther visited me in a dream. Her voice flared inside of mine, or I dreamed myself back to her.

I'm helping her across the street. The street isn't busy, but the busy is inside me, inside her.

We've stepped out from behind a UPS truck onto a small, two-lane country road, and I am stepping out of myself.

The road has no shoulder, but there's no traffic—no need to worry.

It's daylight dim, everything steely, awash in gray, metallic and unnatural. Our skin is ashen. The only bright is the thick dotted line down the center of the road, the classic yellow.

I'm helping Esther by holding on to her arm. She's more wobbly, less sure, more decrepit than I have ever seen her in life, and I notice she can barely walk, so I know my arm is necessary, vital, for her to cross.

Nothing much happens. She doesn't speak. Though I'm supporting her, she's weightless. Within minutes, we're across the road and she vanishes.

In the morning, I chronicled my dream to Myron over coffee.

What I didn't say was that I was tired, the thousands of pages of notes and hundreds of thousands of pages of reading and years of traveling and digging and interviewing, and I wanted her to release me.

But the deep-down part of me understood: Esther wasn't pursuing me with her story; I was chasing her to find mine. Now all I had to do was help her to the other side.

34 Coda

A cloud hovers over the Bitterroots, blows open. Connie emerges.

She finds herself an overhang of sparkling gray granite and a ghost log decaying into the ground. She can lie across the log, the overhang providing shelter from weather, and still see the outline of the mountain ash, the thigh-high mock orange, the wind-slanted elderberry, the drop of rainwater hanging from a huckleberry leaf.

As hours tick by, the smell of damp earth, spruce sap, pine resin comes. Ace snuggles into her. She hears the cry of the cedar waxwing, the scolding Steller's jay, the chortle of the owl, the lovely Swainson's thrush—her favorite—and the traffic of creeks. The constellations shine down on her.

A day passes, and another, and other scents arrive: cougar urine, elk adrenaline, the thread of spiders. Ravens wing overhead.

Ace, throat dry and heart throbbing, creeps away.

Weeks pass and she lifts off on the backs of blowflies, bellies of beetles, teeth of mites. Slime, leaves, and needles cover the log along with bacteria, yeasts, and nematodes.

After another week, snow blankets the log. Wolves and raccoons saunter by.

Months elapse and the log becomes a knowing field.

A mariposa lily takes root, a maidenhair fern. Nuthatches, chickadees, and swifts alight and stay awhile. Martens and squirrels make homes in the log. A black bear digs in looking for ants.

One day a momma moose noses into the log and her brain registers something familiar.

Years pass, and bits of the log make their way to Highline Creek and Parsons Creek. Aquatic fungi, algae, and invertebrates take up residence.

Some of the wood forms small dams, where Chinook salmon rest and forage on their way upstream to mate and die.

Some of the wood shards float to the Selway, the Clearwater, the Snake, the Columbia, where kingfishers and eagles perch.

Other pieces drift to the Pacific Ocean and sink to the sandy bottom. During winter storms limpets and snails move in.

And some stay afloat, traveling thousands of miles.

Decades pass, then centuries, and she feels herself on wings or taking root, cycling through earth, ocean, river, and air, turning and returning, giving rise to new worlds.

Big Rock. 1980. Dick Walker photo.

Acknowledgments

The stories in this book reflect my recollection of events. A few names and identifying characteristics have been changed to protect the privacy of those depicted. Dialogue has been recreated from memory, from notes, and in some cases from digital recordings I made with signed permission from the speakers. From start to finish, this book took over fifteen years to write. Through these years, my husband Myron Lee was an unfailing source of inspiration and support. My daughter Steph Lee, my parents Dennis and Shirley Wagoner, and my brothers Rick, Mike, and Rob Wagoner also encouraged me in important ways. Many people read drafts of this book and gave me generous and incisive feedback: Laura Gephart, Scott Slovic, Vimi Bajaj, Mary Clearman Blew, Rochelle Smith, Jeff Jones, Anne Horowitz, Jennie Nash, Dan Crissman, Temma Ehrenfeld, Josh Dolezal, Rachel Stout, Meredith Tennant, James Lewis, Tom Jenks; my Bennington Writing Seminar teachers Dinah Lenney, Sven Birkerts, Philip Lopate, David Gates, and Wyatt Mason; and scores of others. I'm especially indebted to Joy Passanante and Peter Chilson. One catalyst for this book was the Selway-Bitterroot History Project, for which the National Endowment for the Humanities, Washington State University, and the Idaho Humanities Council provided invaluable support, as did my co-workers Dennis Baird, Devin Becker, Jim Trout, Ben Bunting, Erin Jepsen, and the fifty people who sat for oral history interviews, especially Vernon Carroll and Connie Johnson. The Idaho and Montana Wilderness communities and the Selway-Bitterroot Frank Church Foundation afforded me opportunities to learn about the natural and cultural history of the land, in particular Connie and Lloyd Johnson, Jane Holman, Sarah Walker, Rob Mason, Anna Bengston, Cindy Schacher, Beth Erdey,

Trevor Bond, Matt Root, and Amelia Hagen-Dillon, who designed the map (carincarto.com). For backpacking, riding horse and mule, and flying into the wilderness with me time and again, I thank Peter Chilson, Herb Kittelmann, Cecil Giscombe, Larry Spurgeon, Doug Mackie, Larry Hufford, Ray Hanby, Karen Houppert, Marge and Mark Tabor, the Bitch Lake Women, Dick Walker, Joe Reimensberger, and my family, to name a few. I feel incredibly fortunate to work with the bighearted and whip-smart editors and marketers at Oregon State University Press: Mary Braun, Marty Brown, Micki Reaman, Tom Booth, and Kim Hogeland. I'm reminded of how many people across the United States and the world devote their lives to preserving wild places—my deepest gratitude to all those dedicated souls.